INWARDIZING RILKE'S DOG OF DIVINE INSEEING INTO ITSELF

Inwardizing Rilke's Dog of Divine Inseeing into Itself

The Dog That Is Not a Dog

Greg Mogenson

A title in the monograph series of The International Society for Psychology as the Discipline of Interiority, vol. 5.

Published by
Dusk Owl Books
London, Ontario, Canada

Cover design and typesetting by
Michael Mendis

ISBN 978-1-9992266-3-3

Contents

ACKNOWLEDGEMENTS

A shorter version of the first essay of this volume was presented as a talk at a conference of The International Society for Psychology as the Discipline of Interiority that was held at the Chestnut Conference Centre, Toronto, Ontario, July 21, 2013. Divided into two parts, the full version of the essay was then published as "Inwardizing Rilke's dog of 'divine inseeing' into itself," *Journal of Analytical Psychology*, 2015, volume 60, issue 2, pp. 245-266 and "The bark and bite of the logically negative soul: further reflections on Rilke's dog of 'divine inseeing,'" *Journal of Analytical Psychology*, 2015, volume 60, issue 2, pp. 267-280.

The second essay of this volume, "The dog that is not a dog: a rejoinder to Stanton Marlan," was published in the *International Journal of Jungian Studies,* 2017, volume 9, issue 1, pp. 42-57. In it is offered a critical response to Marlan's, "The absolute that is not absolute: An alchemical reflection on the caput mortuum, the dark other of logical light," *International Journal of Jungian Studies*, 2016. doi:10.1080/19409052.2016.1237372.

For Dr. Marlan's spirited reply to this volume's second essay, see his article, "Response to Greg Mogenson. My dog that is not my dog: the slippery slope of PDI as a method of psychology. *International Journal of Jungian Studies,* 2017, volume 9, issue 1, pp. 58-61.

G. M.

SOURCES AND ABBREVIATIONS

The following abbreviations have been used for frequently cited sources:

CEP: Wolfgang Giegerich, *The Collected English Papers of Wolfgang Giegerich*, 6 vols., New Orleans: Spring Journal Books, 2005-2013. Cited by volume and page number.

CW: Carl Gustav Jung, *Collected Works*, 20 vols. Herbert Read, Michael Fordham, Gerhard Adler and William McGuire, eds., R. F. C. Hull, trans., Princeton: Princeton University Press, 1957-1979. Cited by volume and paragraph number.

MDR: C. G. Jung, *Memories, Dreams, Reflections.* Rev. ed., Aniela Jaffé. Trans. Richard and Clara Winston. New York: Vintage Books, 1989, cited by page number.

Spring: *Spring: A Journal of Archetype and Culture*, New Orleans: Spring Journal Books. Cited by year, in some cases by volume number.

Inwardizing Rilke's Dog of "Divine Inseeing" into Itself

Rilke's Dog, Jung's Pig

I BEGIN WITH A QUOTATION from a letter of Rilke's in which the imaginal acuity of the poet—or to use his term for this, "inseeing"—is described and celebrated:

> I love inseeing. Can you imagine with me how glorious it is to insee, for example, a dog as one passes by. To insee (I don't mean inspect, which is only a kind of human gymnastic, by means of which one immediately comes out again on the other side of the dog, regarding it merely, so to speak, as a window upon the humanity lying behind it, not that)—but to let oneself precisely into the dog, the place in it where God, as it were, would have sat down for a moment when the dog was finished, in order to watch it under the influence of its first embarrassments and inspirations and to know that it was good that nothing was lacking, that it could not have been better made … Laugh though you may, dear confidant, if I am to tell you where my all-greatest feeling, my world-feeling, my earthly bliss was to be found, I must confess to you; it was to be found time and again, here and there, in such timeless moments of divine inseeing.[1]

A beautiful passage! Immediately evocative of the poetic sensibility that Rilke wants to convey, it at the same time, and just as evocatively, presents what in psychology has been called the challenge of the Entrance Problem.[2] Rilke, as he says, loves

[1] R. M. Rilke's letter to Magda von Hattingberg, 17 February, 1914. Quoted by J. B. Leishman in the Introduction to his translation of Rainer Maria Rilke, *New Poems*. London: The Hogarth Press, Ltd. 1964, pp. 18-19.

inseeing. His "all-greatest feeling," "world-feeling," and "earthly bliss" consists in his getting into the phenomenon at hand, in his example, into "a dog as one passes by." But how is this achieved? How does one, as he puts it, "let oneself precisely into the dog, [into] the place in it where God, as it were, would have sat down for a moment when the dog was finished, in order to watch it under the influence of its first embarrassments and inspirations and to know that it was good that nothing was lacking, that it could not have been better made ... " This is the question that I propose to take up in the following reflections.

But first a word about the relation of psychology and poetry. From as early as Freud's "Poets and Daydreaming," psychoanalysis has drawn inspiration from poetry. In the Jungian tradition we have only to think of Jung's seminal essays, "Analytical Psychology and its Relation to Poetry" and "Psychology and Literature." Arguing in these articles against a reductive, personalistic approach to poetry, Jung emphasizes instead the spiritual might of the poetic imagination. Visionary poetry, in his view, is expressive of the heights and depths of the human soul, or as he conceptualized this, of the collective unconscious. Rather than reducing such poetry to the poet as a man or woman, he stressed instead its transcending character. It was not, in his view, the poet Goethe who created his poem, *Faust*, but *Faust* that created Goethe. A wonderful insight![3] As a topic and possible subject matter of psychology, the visionary poetry discussed by Jung is not to be explained or explained away by psychology. It is rather the other way around. Inspired by the interpretative challenge that such poetry presents, psychology finds itself compelled to redefine its

---

2 The title of the conference that a shorter version of this essay was presented at was "The Entrance Problem of Psychology." See Acknowledgments page above for more information.

3 C. G. Jung, CW 15 ¶ 159. While this is indeed a wonderful insight, considered in the light of the conception of interiority being explored in these pages we have to realize that Jung reduced the poetry to the personal after all, inasmuch as his conception of persons was that each one had in his inner a collective unconscious.

concept of the psychological, its concept of itself. Or so in Jung's wake, James Hillman was subsequently to argue. Taking Jung's insight regarding poetry as the starting point of his own project and continuing it more radically, Hillman reconceived psychology in the Jungian tradition as springing from what he called "a poetic basis of mind."[4] Psychoanalysis, in his view, was to be practiced without a patient.[5] Even when it had one—and Hillman, of course, was a practicing analyst—its main effort could be conceived of as a delving into the psychology of the image without explanatory recourse to what is already known about the man or woman who had brought it to the hour in a personal sense. And then there is the approach of Giegerich and PDI.[6] Deeply informed by the earlier contributions of Jung and Hillman, it has been Giegerich's distinction to have taken the further step of interiorizing the various phenomena that they were able to conceive as poetical image each one more deeply into itself via a reiterative process of immanent critique which he called "thinking the image" as opposed to merely imagining along with it. Just as the philosopher in Plato's allegory of the cave is the one who does not fall for the shadows on the cave wall, but performs an about-turn, so psychology, while working with images, does not simply fall for their natural looks, but performing an *opus contra naturam,* discerns and above all *thinks* the contradictions that are involved in the imagination's conceit of passing its mindedness off as if it were but the passive witness of the natural world. And in this context we may cite the alchemical dictum,

---

[4] James Hillman, *Archetypal Psychology: A Brief Account.* Dallas, Spring Publications, 1983, pp. 6-10.

[5] James Hillman, "Bachelard's *Lautréamont.* Or, Psychoanalysis without a Patient" in Gaston Bachelard, *Lautréamont.* Dallas: The Dallas Institute Publications, 1986, pp.103-123.

[6] The acronym refers to "psychology as the discipline of interiority," an approach to analytical psychology stemming from the writings of Wolfgang Giegerich. See especially his *The Soul's Logical Life: Towards a Rigorous Notion of Psychology*, Frankfurt am Main: Peter Lang GmbH, 1998.

"*quod natura relinquit imperfectum ars perficit*"—"What nature leaves imperfect, the art perfects."

With this brief account of the affinity between depth psychology and poetry in mind, we may now return to our passage from Rilke. It is readily apparent that what Rilke wants to describe is a poetic sensibility that can see its subject matter from within. With regards to his example of "a dog as one passes by," such seeing or "inseeing" as he calls it (from the German *einsicht*, which can also be translated as "insight") is not a matter of "inspecting" the dog from an external, human vantage point, but of seeing by means of the dog's absolute inherence in the full coordinated array of features and situation that make it the dog that God, as it were, made it to be. Now this, of course, has long been mankind's job description. Indeed, we may be reminded by the distinction the poet draws between an internal viewpoint described as God's, on the one hand, and our external, human vantage point, on the other, of Adam in the Book of Genesis having been assigned by God the task of naming the animals in Eden.[7] The poet, as Rilke here describes him, is a sort of continuation of Adam even as the verses poets write reach back to and carry on from the Word that was "In the beginning … ," according to the first line of John's gospel.[8] And in this connection it is interesting to note that during a sterile period in which he was blocked in his writing, the fallen Rilke, if I may call him that, restored himself as a poet by visiting the Paris Zoological Gardens, on the advice of the sculptor Auguste Rodin, with whom he was closely associated, to observe the animals.

But here the question arises: can what is fallen truly be restored? Can one really, once the animals have been named, once there is language and poetry, return to immediacy, i.e., to the inseeing that Rilke celebrates? In the Book of Genesis the fall of Adam and Eve was brought about by their sin of eating the fruit

[7] Genesis 2:20.
[8] John 1:1.

of the Tree of the Knowledge of Good and Evil which had been forbidden to them. But was their fall not just as much brought about by the linguistic turn of Adam's having named the animals—a matter of a self-negation?

In one of his *Visions Seminars,* Jung makes his own case for what Rilke called inseeing. In a passage in which he addresses the topic of "assimilating one's own animal nature," the great psychologist states, "We have an entirely wrong idea of the animal; we must not judge from the outside. From the outside you see a pig covered with mud and wallowing in dirt … that pig from outside is dirty … for you it would be dirty, but it is not for the pig. What you have to do is put yourself inside the pig."[9] With these lines Jung makes common cause with Rilke. The point about seeing from within is the same for both of them, only the critter is different. And there is common cause as well with PDI. Conceived as the discipline of interiority, our psychology harkens back to this passage. In his writings Giegerich cites it again and again, not for the meaning it has in its specific context in Jung's text—that of returning to the nature in ourselves, or as he puts it, "assimilating one's own animal nature"—but for what it intimates concerning the stance of interiority that psychology must take if there is to be psychology in the first place. According to Giegerich and PDI, psychology is about seeing, or better, comprehending the phenomena which it takes up as its subject matter, not from any of the many possible external vantage points which might be adopted, but from within.

But what does this mean, "seeing from within"? And how is such inwardness achieved? Neither of our passages gives any thought to the topic of this conference, what Giegerich has called "The Entrance Problem."[10] Rilke simply speaks with delight about

---

[9] C. G. Jung, *Visions: Notes of the Seminar given 1930—1934*, ed. Claire Douglas, 2 vols, Bollingen Series, Princeton: Princeton University Press, p. 168.

[10] For more on the entrance problem see Wolfgang Giegerich, *The Soul's Logical*

his poetic proclivity to get inside the passing dog, Jung of our having to put ourselves inside the pig. Just like that, they are inside.

Or are they?! Much as I value the references Rilke and Jung make to interiority in these passages, I have to own to some doubts about these. How facilely they speak of attaining the stance of interiority! Why, it is as if interiority or "the soul" could be accessed directly, without mediation. Do the poet and the psychologist think themselves still residents of Eden? Is what they give out as interiority not a naïve, faulty version of this, not interiority at all, but rather an erstwhile attempt to restore the immediacy and unbroken unity of the *unio naturalis* and the natural mind?

Earlier I spoke of Adam naming the animals. I suggested that the linguistic turn represented by that passage in the Eden story, if I may anachronistically call it that, was *already the Fall*—the Fall, that is to say, out of immediacy and into reflectedness. Making a similar point Hegel famously declared that "The name is … the thing so far as it exists and counts in the ideational realm." "Given the name lion, we need neither the actual vision of the animal, or its image even: the name alone, if we *understand* it, is the unimaged simple representation. We *think* in names."[11]

Like Hegel's "lion," so also Rilke's "dog" and Jung's "pig." Having long ago been named by our ancestors if not by Adam, they are *not* the immediate presences that Rilke and Jung had fancied them to be, not even the ones right there barking and oinking in front of us. On the contrary, "the dog as one passes by," the pig that wallows in the dirt, have already passed through the mind

---

Life, Frankfurt am Main, Peter Lang GmbH, 1989, chapter one, "No Admission!"

[11] G. W. F. Hegel, *The Encyclopaedia of the Philosophical Science*, part III, § 462 and note. In these lines Hegel distinguishes thinking in names from intuitional and image-based cognition, but does not yet indicate how thinking in names actually thinks. What thinking in names consists in, amounts to, and means becomes clearer, however, when the move away from intuition and image to name-thinking is read in relation to his introduction of the speculative proposition into philosophy. This topic is discussed in detail later in this essay.

countless times. They are already sublated, already concept, already psychology, even.

We may be reminded in this connection of an exchange between James Hillman and Wolfgang Giegerich that took place in the late 1980s in the pages of *Spring Journal.*[12] In the course of promoting the antique idea of the *anima mundi* as a viable notion with respect to our world-relation today, Hillman had spoken of cultivating a complementary aesthetic sensibility for which even "the icy wind that strikes one's chest and disturbs the [cigarette] butts in an ashtray," to take but one example, is "an event directly sensible, directly impinging as a self-display."[13] Having none of this, Giegerich critically responds:

> The icy wind that strikes my chest and disturbs the butts in an ashtray is … not simply an "event directly sensible, directly impinging as a self-display." Our sensation is not all that innocent anymore. It has been affected by and gone through numerous mediations and retains, as *aufgehoben*, within itself a long history of imagination, enlightenment, re-imagination, new enlightenment and all the tears and scars that go along with it, even if all this lies completely under the surface. The icy wind too is mended, if not rent (which, according to Heidegger's Hegel, would be the better state). We cannot sense the wind as the pre-Homeric Greeks did. We cannot undo the fact that ours are eyes that have looked through telescopes and microscopes and into television tubes and have been in museums and seen thousands of posters, art reproductions, statistical charts and scientific diagrams; and ears that have listened to motors, to the rumble of cannons, to string quartets and rock, to digitalized music. We cannot undo the fact that we know about sound and light waves. …. under these conditions the idea of the directly sensible wind—just like that, without further ado—is a cozy idea that misses what is to be seen or felt today, misses *today's* self-display and poetry in the things of

[12] In an article titled, "Hegel, Giegerich and the U.S.A.," published in *Spring 1988*, Hillman responded to Giegerich's *Spring 1987* article, "The Rescue of the World. Jung, Hegel and the Subjective Universe." Giegerich, in turn in the same volume, then responded to Hillman's article with an essay titled, "Effort? Yes, Effort!"

[13] James Hillman, "Hegel, Giegerich and the U.S.A.," *Spring 1988*, p. 178.

> nature: the wind, the tree, the bush, the doe are rent, scarred, even dead; they are ghosts of what they once were.[14]

Giegerich's critique of Hillman's supposedly *anima mundi*-restoring aesthetic sensibility could be applied as well to the passages we have cited from Rilke and Jung. For if, as he put it, "the wind, the tree, the bush, the doe are rent, scarred, even dead; … ghosts of what they once were," so too are the poet's dog and the psychologist's pig. And in this connection, I am reminded of a twist Giegerich gives to a statement of Jung's. In a passage in which he discusses the primitive idea of "loss of soul," Jung states that the primitive mind conceived that variety of psychopathological states which are characterized by a "diminution of personality" (perhaps like what we now call depression, depersonalization, or schizoid withdrawal) via "the supposition that a soul has gone off, just like a dog that runs away from his master overnight. It was then [Jung adds] the task of the medicine-man to fetch the fugitive back."[15] Doubtless, this is an apt description of the primitive situation. And further to this we can suspect that Jung's discussion of the importance of our "assimilating our own animal nature," leading as this does to his mentioning the different perspective that is to be gained by getting inside the pig, is his analyst's version of the medicine-man's fetching back the lost soul. But there is a rather different insight to be had here, a different inseeing. As Giegerich taking Jung's discussion of the primitive "loss of soul" idea a little further points out, "… it is precisely only through its loss, its absence, that the soul first makes itself felt. Just as we become aware of the air around us when it is used up, when we run out of breath, or fear to suffocate, but not when everything is normal, so the soul, when it is 'present' (or rather *merely* '*not* lost') is not experienced as such at all. Its 'loss' is

[14] Wolfgang Giegerich, "Effort? Yes, Effort!" *Spring 1988*. Now in *CE P.* vol. IV, pp. 68-69. As was mentioned in an earlier footnote, Hillman's paper, "Hegel, Giegerich, and the USA," was published in the same volume of *Spring Journal.*

[15] C. G. Jung, *CW* 9i ¶ 213.

the first immediacy of an awareness of soul (as a sense of 'me')—which is another indication of the soul's negativity."[16] And then, specifically drawing upon Jung's line about the soul having run away like a dog from its master in the night he writes, "Only when 'the dog' has run away from his master, only when 'the soul bird' has flown away [from out of the mouth of the dead man], do the dog and the bird come into being and *are* they soul in the first place, but not when they are with their master."[17]

With these reflections, I believe, I have shown Rilke's passage about inseeing and Jung's about entering the pig to be faulty, naïve. When rigorously interrogated what they in these passages give out as interiority has rather to do with a cheery and facile reaching after immediacy and a restoration of the *unio naturalis.* This, however, was not the poetic sensibility that informed Rilke when he composed his greatest poems. Those poems were written after periods of seeming sterility and writer's block. They were written not from within the dog of inseeing, but—if I may put it this way—from within the absence of that dog, from out of that dog's having run away. In the first lines of the *Duino Elegies*, for example, inspiration is not accessed via the traditional invocation of the muse, but from an invocation of the *departedness* of that spirit, the *departedness* of that soul. "If I cried out / who would hear me up there / among the angelic orders?"[18] The poet is alone, without immediate religious and metaphysical resources. As one who knows of air by having run out of it, so via a similar negation does Rilke gain access to his true inspiration. "Throw armfuls of emptiness / out to the spaces / that we breathe— / maybe the birds / will sense / the expanded air / flying more fervently."[19] And the same can be said of Jung. It was not out of his

---

[16] Wolfgang Giegerich, *What Is Soul?* New Orleans: Spring Journal Books, 2012, p. 262.

[17] Giegerich, *What Is Soul?*, p. 262.

[18] Rainer Maria Rilke, *Duino Elegies*, trans. David Young, New York: W. W. Norton & Company, 1978, 1st Elegy, p. 19.

[19] Rilke, *Duino Elegies*, trans. David Young, 1st Elegy, p. 19.

entering the pig in the manner he so facilely describes that his psychology came (insist though he did upon the immediate availability of what he called "God's World" even into the reminiscences of his old age[20]), but out of the *departedness* of the very soul tradition which he sought to restore by such means. As he himself expresses this in a well-known passage, "All ages before us have believed in gods in some form or other. Only an unparalleled impoverishment of symbolism could enable us to rediscover the gods as psychic factors, that is, as archetypes of the unconscious."[21]

But what does it mean, "departedness"? What does it mean, "dog in its negativity"?

I said that our passages from Rilke and Jung present inseeing and interiority in a faulty manner. In them (and I am only talking of these particular passages) the interiority that inseeing is about is merely discussed from the outside. While being preached to the reader, it is not applied to itself. This shows in the fact that what is taken up as the subject matter is in fact quite arbitrary. The way Rilke speaks of the dog, Jung of the pig, they could just as well have spoken of some other creature or thing. Their entering into the dog as one passes by, or into a pig as it wallows in the dirt, is at most a literal getting inside something that then surrounds as an outside. The problem with this, however, is that an aloofness remains. The notion of interiority does not itself pass into itself, is not applied to itself, by way of the specifics of the phenomenon at hand. It remains unscathed. True interiority, by contrast, leaves the outside behind. It meets itself in its other, as its other, itself a second time. Hillman in working out his psychology of the image introduced the important distinction that an image is not an image *of* a dog or *of* a pig, but an image *as* dog, *as* pig.[22]

[20] C. G. Jung, *MDR*, p. 72.

[21] C. G. Jung, *CW* 9, ¶ 50.

[22] James Hillman, "Further Notes on Images," *Spring 1978*, p. 173: "But an image is not an image *of* an object. It images itself. It imagines; and, in its imagining, whatever objects, whatever they are—lemons on a plate, sister in a Chevy—now become imaginational, parts of the image, as if painted, as if dreamt."

It is the same with inseeing, interiority, or the soul. True interiority is not the inside of some positively-existing thing. It is not like God's getting inside his creation such that he is then encased within it. Rather, sublated from the outset, it comes *as those things*—as those things, that is to say, inasmuch as they already bear and bring to bear the mindedness of the mind.

"Our gold is not the people's gold," declares the familiar alchemical dictum. Likewise, our dog is not the people's dog, our pig not the people's pig. But rather and on the contrary, like the alchemical stone that is not a stone, ours is a dog that is *not a dog*, a pig that is *not a pig*.

The insight to be grasped here is that the stance of interiority is not established, nor its notion fulfilled, by our climbing from outside into something. While this, to be sure, is how we imagine it to be, drawing upon our visual knowledge of the world, with the advance to *thinking interiority* we realize that it is nothing else but its presentation of itself to itself *as* dog, *as* pig, or whatever the phenomenon may be. Drawing upon Hegel via Giegerich, what we in PDI call "absolute negative interiorization" is simply the realization that the soul is *speaking about itself* via the phenomenon at hand. Speaking always and exclusively about itself, to itself, the soul IS interiority, not the interiority *of* some creature or thing, but interiority *as* that creature, *as* that thing. And here I am reminded of a distinction drawn by Giegerich. "Psychology," he writes, "is the study of the reflection in some mirror and not the study of what the mirror is the reflection of."[23] The phenomenon at hand—be it a dog, a pig, or whatever else—has for psychology the character of a mirror and, in keeping with this, our interest is in the specifics of that reflectedness in each particular case, and not in what the mirror is a reflection of.

---

[23] Wolfgang Giegerich, "Is the Soul 'Deep?' Entering and Following the Logical Movement of Heraclitus' 'Fragment 45'," *Histories-Spring 64* (1998), pp. 1-2. Also published in *CEP* IV, p. 132.

How else could it be? We already know from Hillman and Giegerich's "icy wind" debate, that Rilke's dog and Jung's pig are "… not simply … event[s] directly sensible, directly impinging as a self-display." We already know that our apprehension of them, of anything, is a function of "a long history of imagination, enlightenment, re-imagination, new enlightenment and all the tears and scars that go along with it …" Taking this a little further we can also see—and this, I maintain, is the real inseeing—that inasmuch as they body-forth this history, they are in this their departedness like letters and words, figurative and linguistic. "Everything we can possibly know and experience," writes Giegerich,

> consists of soul stuff, has been filtered through language and images. We touch an oak tree and think that we touch the real thing, but what we touch is 'oak tree,' which is a human concept and image. We see a cow, a mountain, the moon, a fog, my mother, but all these perceptions are linguistic and mental concepts. Even the idea of something incomprehensible and the idea Jung toyed with … of an extra-linguistic reality as an absolutely unknowable X ('the essence of things external to ourselves') *is a linguistic concept.* There is for us no exit from the soul, the soul in this general sense, and soul is here synonymous with consciousness.[24]

It is all soul stuff, writes Giegerich. The dog as one passes by, the pig in the dirt, have been filtered through language, mediated by a plethora of words and images. And we can turn this around. Dog and pig are for the mind that named them its letters and words. That is to say, as reflections in some mirror their signifying power outstrips what they literally, empirically, naturalistically are. Up from Eden bearing Adam's names (as well a host of others, from Lassie and Rin-Tin-Tin to The Three Little Pigs), they come to the poet, the psychologist, and to the plain man in poetic or psychologically important moments, as figures of meaning to begin with.

---

[24] Giegerich, *What Is Soul?*, p. 75.

And this is so even *before* any of this is made explicit through our actually speaking. Even before the poet's verse or the psychologist's interpretation, the event itself, in the way that it happens, whispers its soul-meaning inasmuch as the consciousness that it simultaneously appears to, bodies forth, and exists as is already implicitly linguistic.

The dog as one passes by, the pig in the dirt, these and all the rest would not come to our attention, would not become topics for us at all, if their Being were not in some soulful sense in excess of their mere factual taking up space and existing. As Giegerich avers, "Psychological phenomena are *events of meaning.* ... to be events of meaning is their nature." And "'events of meaning' means that psychic occurrences are in themselves fundamentally linguistic (linguistic *as events*, i.e., ever prior to and without being put into words)."[25]

Of course, the fundamentally linguistic character of psychic events discussed here by Giegerich has much to do with the aforementioned "long history of imagination, enlightenment, re-imagination, new enlightenment and all the tears and scars that go along with it..." There are, however, other aspects as well. Psychic events are also linguistic in the sense of Hegel's "speculative sentence." In his *The Phenomenology of Spirit,* Hegel discusses how people often complain that they have to read philosophical sentences again and again.[26] This, he claims, does not necessarily show up something faulty about these sentences. On the contrary, it is essential to, the driver of, their speculative power. While in ordinary straightforward sentences something additional to the sentence subject is given in the predicate (for example, the subject is said to have done something, to have some quality, or gone through

[25] Wolfgang Giegerich, "The Sacrifice of Isaac and the Watershed of History," in *C.E.P.* Vol. III, p. 175.

[26] G. W. F. Hegel, *The Phenomenology of Spirt*, A. V. Miller, trans., Oxford: Oxford University Press, 1977, § 63, p, 39.

some experience), what makes speculative sentences speculative is that the predicate is the subject *once more*, and this moreover in a manner that unsettles and redefines what we had thought the subject to be and the sentence to be about at the outset—hence the need to read and re-read. Well, it is the same with all psychic events. Psychic events are not just things that happen to us as fixed, determinate subjects.[27] They are not merely experiences we as subjects have and take note of in the predicates we trail. No, they are the subject a second time, the mediating *doppelgängers* of our own departedness. And this is so whether one has oneself the place of the sentence subject or, as the case may be, we are dealing with a soul document in which what had seemed on the surface to be its topic or subject matter is being seconded into its self-re-defining, subject-verifying, concept-ratifying depths.

Earlier, I quoted Giegerich's discussion of how we don't know air until we run out of it and along with this his statement about how it is "Only when 'the dog' has run away from his master, only when 'the soul bird' has flown, do the dog and the bird come into being and *are* they soul in the first place, but not when they are with their master." It is the same with our self-experience as subjects in the sense of the speculative sentence. Encountering an Other, any other—a dog as one passes by, a pig wallowing in the dirt, another human being—a negation occurs. Seconded as sentence subjects, we find that we (or the subject matter we are concerned with when this is regarded as having self-character) are *running, not out of air this time, but out of our self-identicalness as subjects!* For the other before us is not merely some external thing over there about which we as fixed subjects can make correct descriptive and identifying statements. It is the subject's own other, that is, the subject a second time, the subject re-defined.[28] And so it is that we gaze into the gaze that

---

[27] Jung, quite erroneously, likened psychic events to bricks that could hit one's head (cf. *MDR*, p. 62).

[28] The words "subject redefined" may put us in mind of the dismemberment

gazes back at us, eye to eye, subject to subject, as if reading the encounter again and again as one must when reading a speculative sentence. And this is also the case for those "selves" that are our topics and subject matters. Leaving ourselves out of the picture, though of course not completely (we only need to be dead to do psychology,[29] not obliterated), soul-documents as various as poems and dreams, symptoms and life-situations may be interiorized into themselves, released re-definitionally into their truth, via the same speculative process of seeing through the looks and glances of their various internal moments even as these are read again and again in terms of the unity of their identity and difference.[30]

* * *

We began with Rilke's text about inseeing. Interiorized into itself, released into its truth or concept, this account, which we readily showed to be a too naïve one, has gone under and across into a more fully speculative poetics. Of course, the text we have been working with was only a letter; some lines dashed off in haste, perhaps. Its being a poor example of what it is actually about could simply be ascribed to this. But even so, and if despite all its merits of beauty and charm, it must be rated a poor example of the "inseeing" it describes, it nevertheless *contains as such* the prospect of

---

motif in mythology. Transposing my criticism of Rilke's text about inseeing into the terms of Giegerich's discussion of the myth of Actaion and Artemis in *The Soul's Logical Life*, pp, 203-275, we could say that Rilke's vision is only the halfway point of that myth. In beholding the dog in the wondrous manner that he describes, Rilke sees, if I may put it this way, the virgin goddess bathing, but has not yet tarried with the negation that the dog mediates and been torn apart by its subject-seconding, essence-adumbrating, speculative meaning. The point to be grasped, however, is that seeing the goddess and being torn apart by the dog(s) are speculatively "the same." This topic will be explored more fully later in this essay.

[29] Giegerich writes that "The art of psychological discourse is to speak as someone already deceased." See his *The Soul's Logical Life*, p. 24.

[30] According to Hegel, truth or the Absolute is "the identity of identity and non-identity." Both opposition and unity are in it.

its own sublation. And in this connection we may be put in mind of Hegel's famous statement about "tarrying with the negative."[31] Just as tarrying with the negative is the way to truth, according to that philosopher, so our tarrying in these pages with the self-negation inherent in Rilke's text about "inseeing" is what has led us to a more truthful presentation of the poetic sensibility of the truly inspired poet, the one who could ask, as Rilke in his great work, the *Duino Elegies*, asks,

> Are we, perhaps, here just for saying: House,/Bridge, Fountain, Gate, Jug, Olive Tree, Window, —/possibly: Pillar, Tower? … for such saying as never before the things themselves hoped so intensely to be.[32]

---

[31] Hegel, *Phenomenology of Spirit*, § 32, p, 19.

[32] Rainer Maria Rilke, *Duino Elegies,* trans. J. G. Leishman and Stephen Spender, New York: W. W. Norton & Company, 1939, p. 75.

INTERIORIZING INTERIORITY INTO ITSELF

Above, I criticized Rilke's presentation of inseeing as being faulty in that it conflated interiority with a fanciful *unio naturalis*-restoring vision of immediate unity regained. Further to this, I questioned both his and Jung's concepts of interiority as these are conveyed by the illustrative passages that I quoted from them. These illustrations, I claimed, were just too facile. There was no sense of what Giegerich calls the entrance problem or entrance challenge in them. For all their aesthetic and sensual appeal, the interiority they describe remains an abstract concept. It does not in either of their respective examples concretely come to be defined or redefined by what is being referred to and talked about, what they predicated of it. While the poet effusively claims to be able to interiorize himself into the dog and the psychologist speaks more soberly of interiorization into a pig, neither give a thought to *interiorizing the concept of interiority into itself* in the particular ways that the dog in the one case and pig in the other would specifically inspire. For this deeper and more thoroughgoing approach to interiority we turned to Hegel's great insight concerning the speculative proposition or speculative sentence. In the *Phenomenology of the Spirit,* Hegel describes how in the course of reading philosophical sentences we come to realize that "... we meant something other than we meant to mean; and this correction of our meaning compels our knowing to go back to the proposition, and understand it in some other way."[33] Putting this another way, he states further that when reading such sentences "Thinking ... loses the firm objective [*gegenständlich*] basis it had in the subject when, in the predicate, it is thrown back onto the subject, and when, in the predicate, it does not return into itself, but into the subject of the content."[34] This, I submit, is the self-negating gateway to true

[33] Hegel, *Phenomenology of Spirit,* § 63, p, 39.

[34] *Ibid.*

interiority. True interiority is a matter of ever and again, on each interpretive occasion, discerning whether interiority is in accord with its concept, i.e., whether it is comprehended in the fullness of its mediated depth. It is a matter of thinking the phenomenon in the speculative manner I have been describing, not merely of following the natural looks of things, imagining them. As Giegerich puts it in a sentence that well-conveys this central thrust of PDI, "... psychology begins where any phenomenon (whether physical or mental, 'real' or fantasy image) is interiorized absolute-negatively into itself, and I find myself in its internal infinity. This is what it takes; psychology cannot be had for less."[35]

With the above reflections in mind, let us now return to our passage from Rilke. While he, as I noted, merely talks about interiorizing himself into the dog, our interest is to show how the interiority he discusses may be *truly* interiorized, not literally—man into the dog—, but *logically* into itself via the mediation provided by the dog that the poet sees and delights in.

So let us begin. What Rilke calls "inseeing" we can call negated seeing, in Hegel's terms, negated sense certainty, and moving on from this, negated perception, even. To get at what this means we need only bear in mind a few things about ordinary seeing and ordinary sense perception. It is with our senses that we see, or in Rilke's word "inspect," that which has drawn our attention as an empirical object or thing. From this we get at most a list of correct quality predicates of the phenomenon at hand regarded as a thing, not the essential predicates of the self-intuiting soul. The dog, for example, is big. It wags its tail. It likes to fetch a stick. If, however, we want to get to truth and soul this requires "inseeing," negated seeing, which for us means "thought." Conveying something of this, Rilke speaks of our letting ourselves "… precisely into the dog, [into] the place in it where God, as it were, would have sat down for

---

[35] Giegerich, "Is the Soul 'Deep'?—Entering and Following the Logical Movement of Heraclitus' 'Fragment 45'," p. 31. Also, in *CEP* IV, pp. 161-162.

a moment when the dog was finished, in order to watch it under the influence of its first embarrassments and inspirations and to know that it was good that nothing was lacking, that it could not have been better made ..." But a complication arises here, more than that, a contradiction. Taking our passage seriously we find that what Rilke calls "inseeing" is not as straightforward as his imagery suggests. Though we are supposed to "insee" the dog by means of the poet's appeal to God's supposed mode of inwardizing himself into that creature, the problem with this is that we can almost see with the imagination's semblance of our ordinary eyes (that is, with our sensory intuition) God entering into the dog and sitting in him like one might sit in the cockpit of a sports car! But to sit in something—be it a sports car or a dog—is not truly to be in it. For to be inside in this way is only to be surrounded by something external. Yes, we are in it, but only in such a way that we are still outside. True interiority, by contrast, has nothing surrounding it, nothing external to it. Also called "absolute interiority," it is an interiority that has been *absolved* from the difference between "inner" and "outer." So the point to be grasped is that Rilke's text only *talks about* inseeing; it doesn't really perform it. Unlike the Christian God's emptying himself of his divinity and becoming a man in Christ (Phil. 2:5-8), the God of Rilke's poetic passage is too cumbersome, too tangibly visible, too freighted with imaginal presence of his own to get inside the dog in such a definition re-defining manner.[36] This is the contradiction. True, the line about the place in the dog where God would have sat is very beautiful, but alas, only impotently so, or so I claim with Hegel's line about "Impotent beauty hat[ing] the understanding for asking of her what she cannot do"[37] in mind. The passage is merely a visual aid

[36] As was the dove in my book, *The Dove in the Consulting Room: Hysteria and the Anima in Bollas and Jung*, Hove and New York: Brunner-Routledge, 2003! On this point see the excerpt from a personal letter from Giegerich on pp. 190-191 of that book.

[37] Hegel, *Phenomenology of Spirit* § 32, p. 19.

that represents an absolute negative interiorization which it is unable to perform.

So what, then, is true inseeing? Our critique of Rilke's little piece on this topic is a good example. By showing that its imagery is not up to what it claims to convey, we absolute negatively interiorize, not God into the dog, but the poetic passage into itself, releasing thereby "inseeing" more truly into its concept.

Interiority, inseeing, or the soul is a matter of reading and re-reading. In approaching our text we must read it in such a way that we thinkingly grasp the unity of the identity and difference of its figures in and for the mind. Appearing in the same passage, "God" and "dog" are part and parcel of one another. There is not first a dog and then God, or vice versa, in an external relation. These, rather, and the poet's "I" as well, are moments of the same idea or thought, just as the letters that make up a word are moments of that word or the words that make up a sentence are moments of that sentence. And this means that we must read them, think them, in the light of one another, as if they were interchangeably the subject and essential predicate of a speculative sentence. Never mind that their looks are so different. The letters of the alphabet look different, too. What matters is their mutually appearing as they have only in and through each other. By the same logic that we find in the adages, "birds of a feather flock together" or "it takes one to know one," the appearing together of God and dog may prompt us to say that "God *is* dog," or by the same token, "Dog *is* God."[38]

But what does this mean? The thought as which the soul produces itself in this our moment of interpretative challenge is the thought that is able to grasp that while "dog," "God," and the

---

[38] "Dog is God," and vice versa, recalls Hegel's more general speculative statement, "the particular is universal," as well as Giegerich's insight that "what at first appears as a content [or object] of consciousness is in truth the seed of what wants to become a new form of consciousness at large." See his "Is the Soul 'Deep?'—Entering and Following the Logical Movement of Heraclitus' 'Fragment 45'." Histories-*Spring 64* (Fall/Winter 1998), p. 19. Also, in *CEP* IV, p. 149.

poet's "I" are certainly different they are also in some concept-deepening or expanding sense *the same.* Putting this another way, we can say that what may be variously referred to as interiority, inseeing, or the soul is that thought that thinks the unity of the unity and difference of subjectivity, universality, and particularity even as in our text this triumvirate corresponds to the poet's I ("I love inseeing"), his reference to God, and to the "dog as one passes by," respectively. And further to this a passage from Giegerich comes to mind,

> The first immediacy of the new form of consciousness always appears as a perceived (imagined) object or content before consciousness, and only by one's devoting oneself without reserve to the study of the content is it possible for this content to slowly "come home" to consciousness in the way indicated, so that it now becomes the very form of consciousness itself and ipso facto disappears as a content "out there."[39]

Reflecting this passage in terms of our text from Rilke, or the other way around, our text from Rilke in the terms of this passage, we can see that "the dog as one passes by" corresponds to what Giegerich refers to as the "perceived (imagined) object or content before consciousness," God's entering into the dog to this dog as "the first immediacy of a new form of consciousness," and "one's devoting oneself without reserve to the study of the content" to the poet's apperception, his "… love of inseeing."

The inseeing that Rilke describes only becomes true inseeing as the first immediacy of what is perceived disappears as a content "out there"—God on the one hand and Dog on the other—and comes to be the very form of that seeing. Likewise, the interiority that PDI is concerned with only comes to be truly that if it is redefined by the subject matter it is concerned with. It is a matter of inseeing or interiority being interiorized into itself in terms of the

[39] Giegerich, *The Soul's Logical Life*, p. 149.

mediation provided by the specific subject matter it has posited itself as. Expressing this in the form of a speculative sentence we could say with reference to our passage from Rilke that inseeing *is* "the dog as one passes by." Or again, that interiority *is* this dog. And this dog-mediated interiority is interiority in a very differently nuanced moment of its concept than the one discussed by Jung that is mediated by the pig wallowing in the dirt.

Perhaps then, and I say this only to bring all this theory a bit more to life, what we are variously calling inseeing, interiority, and the soul is like the relation that the Inuit living in the Arctic once had to snow. Knowing snow from within the Inuit of old had many more names for it than have we who have long been emancipated from snow. In the same way, and apropos the symbolic image of the uroboric serpent that bites into its own tail, the pig wallowing in the dirt and the dog chasing circles after its tail are but different expressions, different names, for psychology's lack of an Archimedean point, figures of its inwardness in this quintessential sense.

And here I am put in mind of Rilke's poem, "The Panther," which was one of the most successful of the so-called "Thing-poems" he wrote, inspired by the visits he made to the *Jardin des Plantes* in Paris. In Stephen Mitchell's translation it reads as follows:

> His vision, from the constantly passing bars, has grown so weary that it cannot hold anything else. It seems to him there are a thousand bars, and behind the bars, no world. As he paces in cramped circles, over and over, the movement of his powerful soft strides is like a ritual dance around a center in which a mighty will stands paralyzed. Only at times, the curtain of the pupils' lifts, quietly—An image enters in, rushes down through the tensed, arrested muscles, plunges into the heart and is gone.[40]

[40] R. M. Rilke, *The Selected Poems of Rainer Maria Rilke*, trans. Stephen Mitchell, New York, Vintage Books, 1989, p. 25.

Heir to the Adam who named the animals in Eden, Rilke trains his poet's gaze upon a panther pacing in its cage. His doing so, however, does not make for the kind of relation that might still have been possible in Eden. The Fall, after all, has long since happened; the gate to Eden has closed. Our sensation and perception, as we heard from Giegerich, "… has been affected by and gone through numerous mediations and retains, as *aufgehoben*, within itself a long history of imagination, enlightenment, re-imagination, new enlightenment and all the tears and scars that go along with it …" For this reason alone, it could be argued, there are bars on the panther's cage. If on another occasion the poet faced a panther in a natural setting (sic!), he still could not undo the fact that he had seen it in zoos, in paintings, read stories about it, and the like. And so, in this regard Rilke's panther is already, some ten years before he wrote of them, like one of those absent angels he questioned calling out to in the first lines of his *Duino Elegies*. Indeed, like them the panther, too, is rent, departed, dead; not an animal in nature, but a figure of the mind. And here while I am mentioning the *Duino Elegies* I might as well also mention those lines from them in which Rilke states that "Beauty is only /the first touch of terror / we can still bear / and it awes us so much / because it so coolly / distains to destroy us./ Every single angel is terrible."[41] The panther in his cage, opening his eyes such that an image entering in "… plunges into the heart and is gone," is already this beauty, this terror, this angel of departedness. And this is even if, disturbed by the poet's description of the panther pacing pointlessly in its cage as the life disappears from its eyes, we probably have to interpret the poem as an allegorical depiction of the nihilistic spirit-(lessness) of Man's modern existence.[42] There

[41] These lines, from David Young's translation, appear early in the first elegy.

[42] In a June 24, 2013 email Giegerich writes, "'The Panther' reveals inseeing, but only inSEEING, not interiority, not thought, no sign of interiority having become

really is, as we learned from Giegerich above, "no exit from the soul."

A moment ago, I mentioned the Inuit and their having had many names for the snow in which they formerly lived on such intimate terms. As poets and psychologists, I said, we too need many names for our inwardness in the soul, many names for what Jung called our lack of an Archimedean point of perspective outside and beyond the psyche.[43] If Rilke's poem, "The Panther," provides a particularly disturbing one of these, being reflective, as I just said, of the nihilistic spirit(lessness) of modern existence, Hesse's *Steppenwolf* and Kafka's *Investigations of a Dog* may readily be claimed as others. And this is to say nothing of Orwell's *Animal Farm*,

---

'the very form of consciousness.' I wonder whether one can say that it does not make for a subject here, object there relation. Yes, the panther, too, is rent, departed, dead. But I do not think that this alone is the reason for the bars. The bars also neatly separate subject and object, they turn the panther into an object of almost scientific study, an object ('*Thing*-poem!) that the poet as subject has before himself in safe distance and as well-circumscribed fact. The poet's gaze is a cold diagnostic one. Is inseeing here not empathetic diagnosis? The bars contained *in* the image reflect Rilke's *own* 'form of consciousness' here. Reminiscent of Husserl's phenomenology: the unbridgeable difference between *noêsis* and *noêma*). I see in this Thing-poem an allegory (!) of modern existence: the panther's circling is no longer uroboric, but senseless, in vain. And the poem ends nihilistically (the last lines literally [translated]: 'goes through the limbs' tensed silence - / and in the heart ceases to be') Absolutely pointless, A great poem, but terrible." This interpretation of Giegerich's I regard as compatible with what I am attempting to show with reference to Rilke's "The Panther." For even while depicting the nihilistic loss of soul which is widely considered to be characteristic of modern existence, the poem does so within the soul, within, that is to say, the soul as it is produced by the methodological stance of a psychology defined as the discipline of interiority. And in this connection let us remember Giegerich's insight, discussed in Part One, "Only when 'the dog' has run away from his master, only when "the soul bird" has flown away [from out of the mouth of the dead man], do the dog and the bird come into being and *are* they soul in the first place, but not when they are with their master." It is the same, I maintain, with Rilke's panther.

[43] Actually, it is not so much that we need to *have* such names for our inwardness in the soul, i.e., for what Jung called psychology's lack of an Archimedean point, but rather to recognize that to exercise such name-giving power is the constituting prerogative (not of the soul we *have*, but) of the soul that we *are*, which is also to say, of our being soul.

Melville's *Moby Dick*,[44] Steinbeck's *The Red Pony* and the rest. But I want to turn to two other passages that have come to my mind. Drawn from the treasury of traditional wisdom, these passages roughly convey what interiorizing interiority into itself via the mediation provided by some particular matter of interest amounts to and means.

> A story is told of the famous mystic Abu Bakr Shibli. After his death in Baghdad in the year 945, Abu Bakr appeared to a friend of his in a dream. The friend asked, "How has God treated you?"
>
> Abu Bakr answered: "As I stood before His throne He asked me, 'Do you know why I have forgiven you?'"
>
> "Because of my good deeds?"
>
> "No," answered God.
>
> "Because I was sincere in my worship?"
>
> "No."
>
> "Because of my pilgrimages, fasts, and prayers?"
>
> "No, not on account of those."
>
> "Well then, was it because of my voyages to acquire knowledge and because I left my home to join the holy."
>
> "No."
>
> Baffled Abu Bakr then declared, "O Lord, these are the deeds that lead to salvation and these I have placed above everything else, and I thought that because of them you would forgive me."
>
> To this the Lord said, "No, not on account of all these actions have I forgiven you."
>
> "O Lord, why then?"
>
> Answering, God said, "Do you remember how on a cold winter day you were walking through the streets of Baghdad, and

---

[44] For a discussion of psychology's notion of interiority in light of the whale that figures in Melville's novel *Moby Dick*, see my "Whaling with Giegerich: The Ahab of the Notion," *Journal of Jungian Theory and Practice*, Vol. 6, No. 1, 2004, pp. 67-83. Having been reminded of this article in our present context, I'll take this opportunity to quote an important line from the novel that I neglected to cite before: "In landlessness alone resides the highest truth." In this image of being without connection to any shore we have the idea of nothing external, of complete immersion, of absolute interiority. As a figuring of psychology's inwardness in the soul, i.e., of its lack of an Archimedean point, however (and here I anticipate what shall be explored below), it is still only implicit; it does not yet have the form of the whale, of Moby Dick.

> you found a kitten that was exhausted from the cold and ran from corner to corner to find shelter from the icy wind, and you had pity on it and picked it up and put it inside your fur and protected it from the bitter cold?"
>
> "Yes, I remember."
>
> And then the Lord said, "Because you had pity on that cat, Abu Bakr, because of *that* I have pity on you."[45]

In this story, of course, it is a kitten that features and not a dog as it had been in Rilke's text. But we get from this kitten another hint about inseeing. Rilke spoke of our letting ourselves "precisely into the dog, [into] the place in it where God, as it were, would have sat down for a moment when the dog was finished, in order to watch it under the influence of its first embarrassments and inspirations and to know that it was good, that nothing was lacking, that it could not have been better made ..." But where does our Persian story locate this place? Well, in the manner of what Hegel called the inverted world, it is inside Abu Bakr's fur coat, in the place he created there as he warmed a little kitten by his heart. Thinking the dialectical reversal that the story implies we can say further to this that the inseeing it performs is not of the kitten per se as an object, but of Abu Bakr himself as the subject a second time. The kitten in the coat: that is the *place in Abu Bakr* where God sat down "to know that nothing was lacking, that [he] could not have been better made." Or again, the kitten in the coat by Abu Bakr's heart is already Abu Bakr inside God's coat by the warmth of God's heart.

Now, the challenge of the story of Abu Bakr is to not read it simply as an illustration of an ethical value or as an ideal of interpersonal conduct, as if it was only a decorative way of stressing the importance of being kind. More deeply comprehended, it has to do with inseeing as "absolute knowing" (if I may here draw upon

---

[45] Cited by Paul Watzlawick, *Ultra-Solutions: How to Fail Most Successfully,* London & New York, W. W. Norton & Company, 1988, pp. 93-94.

that most pertinent Hegelian term). Beyond its message about the value of kindness, I have cited it here because of what it conveys with regards to mediation and speculative reason, what Rilke calls "inseeing." We get from the story a sense of what it means for interiority, inseeing, or "the soul" to take on a more specific and precise meaning as a return from its self-othering into dog or kitten as the case may be. But, alas, while conveying this, the earlier mentioned fault remains that the inseeing depicted is still too sensual, too imagistic, too governed by the spatial imagination to overcome the logic of the inside/outside split that I earlier described as God sitting in the dog as if he were in a sports car. To move from this inSEEing, as it might better be called, to a true inseeing in the sense of speculative thought we must realize that the mystic Abu Bakr Shibli's account from inside his friend's dream of being in God's mercy, even as the kitten he had once held inside his coat had been in his mercy, is not a one-inside-the other (inside-the-other!) relation, but a matter of the fast-influencings and dialectical reversals of all these figures as moments of the thought that endeavours to think the unity of their identity and difference.

Our second passage comes from the Gospel of Matthew, Chapter 25, verses 34-40:

> 34 Then shall the King say unto them on his right hand, Come ye blessed of the Father, inherit the kingdom prepared for you from the foundation of the world:
> 35 For I was hungered, and ye gave me meat: I was thirsty, and ye gave me drink: I was a stranger, and ye took me in:
> 36 Naked, and ye clothed me: I was sick, and ye visited me: I was in prison and ye came unto me.
> 37 Then shall the righteous answer him, saying, Lord, when saw we thee an hungered, and fed *thee*?, and gave *thee* drink?
> 38 When saw we thee a stranger, and took *thee* in? or naked, and clothed *thee*?
> 39 Or when saw we thee sick, or in prison, and came unto thee?

> [40] And the King shall answer and say unto them, Verily I say unto you, Inasmuch as you have done *it* unto one of the least of these my brethren, ye have done *it* unto me.

As with the Persian story, here again with this teaching of Jesus', the challenge is to not simply read it as a moral lesson. Of course, it is that, and profoundly so, but our interest has to do with what it shows regarding the constituting structure, not just of the soul truth that it is, but of soul truths generally. The key here is the last line I have quoted, verse 40, the part where Jesus states, "Verily I say unto you, Inasmuch as you have done *it* unto one of the least of these my brethren, ye have done *it* unto me." Notice that this is pretty much synonymous with what we have been discussing with reference to the speculative proposition or speculative sentence. Why, we can even say that along with the lines building up to it, it is nothing else than a lively portrayal of the speculative proposition.

From our Persian story and the text of Jesus' teaching from Matthew's gospel we readily get a good sense of the speculative meaning of what Rilke, with reference to a dog and God, called "inseeing." It only remains for this to be worked out through our own—or better, the dog figure's own—conceptual labour. Inseeing, or as we might more generally call it, speculative insight, is a matter of what Hegel called "the labour of the concept." Compared to this, the use of such parallels as can be drawn from the treasury of traditional wisdom (what Jung called amplification) is but a labour-saving device. Helpful as they may be for putting us in the ballpark, as it were, of the pertinent soul-meaning (or better: as a reminder of what soul-meaning is like), they do not do away with the necessity of such labour altogether. On the contrary, to get to real interpretative results, i.e., to the present tense of a truth, and above all to thought as the measure of all that it in its implicitness appears to itself as, we must work with what is actually present as our phenomenon or matter of interest, and not rest content with edifying comparisons to something else, born of another time and place.

THE SPECULATIVE TURN

Our topic is "inseeing," or rather, this by such other names as speculative reason, absolute-negative interiorization, or more simply put, psychology. Starting as Rilke does in the passage in which he introduces this term with "a dog as one passes by," it is important to realize that if we be poets or psychologists, such "a dog"[46] is negated and sublated from the outset. It is *not*, that is to say, merely a dog in its factual, biological positivity, but something conceptual, noetic, notional, linguistic. In Rilke's text this is indicated by its being referred to as "*an example*." After asking the correspondent he is writing to if she "can imagine how glorious it is to insee," the poet says, "*for example* a dog as one passes by." Now usually examples are representative instances of something, of some substantial topic or subject matter perhaps. But here "example" refers (if I may put it this way) to what Shakespeare, in a line that David Miller has introduced into our discourse, called the "nothing [that] almost sees miracles."[47] Example in this sense is nothing other than the self-unfolding, self-positing, self-redefining mode of the speculative itself. Just as in speculative sentences the subject does not merely wag that predicate that serves as its tail, but, bow-wow, is just as much wagged by that tail in a subject-seconding manner, so in Rilke's text it is a dog in this speculative sense, a dog that is not a dog (even as alchemy speaks of a "stone that is not a stone"), that exemplifies inseeing. And here I am prompted to recall again that statement of Giegerich's: "The psychological question is not, cannot be, what and how the soul is, but how the soul is reflected in its manifestations. … [P]sychology is

---

[46] We should probably imagine quotation marks around this dog even as in PDI we always have to imagine or actually place quotation marks around all references to "the soul."

[47] David L. Miller, "Nothing Almost Sees Miracles! Self and No-Self in Psychology and Religion," *The Journal of the Psychology of Religion*, 4, 5 (1995-1996), pp. 1-26. The quotation is from *King Lear*, II. 2. line 165.

the study of the reflection in some mirror and not the study of what the mirror is the reflection of."[48]

So it is with a negation that we always start, here with a dog grasped from the outset as mediation, mind, and speculative mirror. Just as the fairy tale motif of the climb up the slippery slope, discussed by Giegerich in *Dialectics & Analytical Psychology*, is not about a literal mountain and how it is to be climbed, our dog, the one we encounter in Rilke's text about inseeing, is not the dog of ordinary sense perception, even though, to be sure, it may seem to start with that inasmuch as such a one had been sighted by the poet.[49] An actual dog can be the object of a practical or a scientific outlook. It can be the dog of a shepherd or of a policeman. It can be a family dog, a household pet, etc. As such, it can be studied by a zoologist like any other animal, and when it is ill, treated by a veterinarian. We are not interested in this dog, neither as poets nor as psychologists. Our interest, rather, is with the true dog, which is also to say, with soul-truths or soul-meanings that *allegorically portray themselves* in canine garb.

This dog, as we already discussed, drawing upon a distinction introduced by Hillman, is not an image *of* a dog, but image *as* dog. And it is this, moreover, in such a manner that it is not visible to the eye except as (always already and now once again) it is *thought* by that "long history of imagination, enlightenment, re-imagination, new enlightenment" that we call the mind. Putting this in terms of the subject/object or subject/predicate distinction, we can say that

---

[48] Giegerich, "Is the Soul 'Deep?', *op. cit.*, pp. 1-2. Also, *CEP* IV, pp. 131-132.

[49] Wolfgang Giegerich, David L. Miller, Greg Mogenson, *Dialectics & Analytical Psychology: The El Capitan Canyon Seminar*, New Orleans: Spring Journal Books, 2005, pp. 1-24. As for the slipperiness—the subtitle of Giegerich's first chapter has the phrase, "and The Climb up the Slippery Slope"—the equivalent of this in our discussion is to be found in the observation that the various examples used in the previous section to convey the interiorization of interiority into itself via a mediating other did not overcome, but fell back behind, the earlier critique of the subject here/object there split and of the God getting inside the dog like He is getting inside a sports car logic.

our dog is not the literal, empirical dog over there objectively in front of us, the subjects (prompted though the self-intuiting soul in us may be by such a dog). It is not, that is to say, merely something external that can be set off from us in the predicate we trail, in the manner, say, of the sentence out of a children's reader, "The man [in addition to being the man that he is] has a dog with him." Nor, by the same token, if the dog itself is regarded as the subject, is it this in a sense that is separable from the qualities and actions that are then attributed to it. On the contrary (and returning to that children's reader), its "See Spot run!" character must be read speculatively. The dog, "Spot," that is to say, does not first exist and then on top of that or in addition to that "run." It is only by virtue of this running that he is the dog that he is and that we know by the name Spot in the first place. The one term or moment "run" is as "essential" as the other moment, "dog" or "Spot."[50] And the same is arguably the case with the earlier sentence, "The man has a dog." A prosaic sentence to be sure, but there may yet be moments of insight or inseeing in which "The man has a dog" is so equally "The dog has a man" that, leaving behind the rank and file or their respective natural species, a new species or rather genus of meaning is neo-logistically established in the mind. It is a matter, as we learned from Giegerich, of reflections that have been absolved from the things they seemed to be the reflection of. And here we may think of that man with a dog, the mythical Actaion, who after glimpsing the Goddess Artemis bathing was turned upon by his own hounds, pursued and torn apart by them. Or taking with Hegel the step beyond such an imagistic figuring of the action of the knowing mind to philosophy and the notion, think again of his great insight about how "Thinking … loses the firm objective

[50] We may recall in this connection the statement from Giegerich that we quoted earlier, "Only when 'the dog' has run away from his master, only when "the soul bird" has flown away [from out of the mouth of the dead man], do the dog and the bird come into being and are they soul in the first place, but not when they are with their master." From *What Is Soul?*, p. 262.

[*gegenständlich*] basis it had in the subject when, in the predicate, it is thrown back on to the subject, and when, in the predicate, it does not return into itself, but into the subject of the content."[51]

I said that examples are in our psychological context nothing other than the self-unfolding, self-positing, self-reflecting and self-redefining mode of the speculative itself. And further to this I just now spoke of these as a new species or genus of meaning that neo-logistically establishes itself in the mind when the unity of the unity and difference of such various moments of reflection as "man", "god," "dog" are *thought.* Examples (of such examples!) are legion. Without troubling ourselves with symbolic references to the dogs that have figured in myth, we can simply think of the ones that figure in familiar idiomatic phrases and adages. I have already mentioned "the tail wags the dog," drawing upon this saying to characterize the reflexive action or logical movement of speculative sentences. Other dog-mediated determinations of inseeing that come readily to mind include "the hair of the dog that bit you," "a barking dog never bites," "I've got to go and see a man about a dog," "a dog in the manger," "dog eat dog," "shaggy dog story," "give a dog a bad name and hang him," "let sleeping dogs lie," and of course, "barking up the wrong tree." Just as in the traditional religious view, all the various creatures and the whole of life even were regarded to have been created to begin with as God's own thoughts (such that there would be no need for God to have then to climb into them in the manner Rilke described!), so the dogs which feature in these idiomatic phrases are indicative of the locutions of our thoughts and minds. It is these—our cognitions, arguments, mental determinations and theses—that often prove to be barking up the wrong tree or that must be hung, as it were, for the wrong names they have barked out.

The point to be grasped here is the same point I made earlier when I said, apropos that old story about Adam and the animals in

[51] Hegel, *Phenomenology of Spirit*, § 62, p, 39.

Eden, that dogs and pigs (and, of course, pretty much everything else) are for the mind that named them its letters and words. Like letters and words, the sayings I have listed have a signifying power that extends far beyond what they might once have been literally derived from. Again, it is not an actual dog barking up the wrong tree that the phrase about it doing so is about. Not an actual dog that is hung for his bad name in the adage that speaks in terms of that imagery. Such sayings serve rather to indicate in an externalizing manner the inwardness of the concept that all that they are not exists as. As Hegel puts it, "We only know our thoughts, only have definite, actual thoughts, when we give them the form of objectivity, of a being distinct from our inwardness, and therefore the shape of externality, and of an externality, too, that at the same time bears the stamp of the highest inwardness. The articulated sound, the *word* [also: name, saying, or adage—G.M.], is alone such an inward externality."[52]

Adapting Rilke's text in the light of this statement, its first line, the one in which the concept of "inseeing" is introduced, can now be read to say, "Can you imagine with me how glorious it is to insee 'an inward externality' as one passes by?" For, again, it is our own thought that we know in the example of a dog as one passes by, our own thinking that is out-pictured in this externalizing *pars pro toto* manner.

From here we can return to the comparison I drew above between psychology's lack of an Archimedean point outside of the soul and the snowy infinity of the arctic tundra which was known by the Inuit living within it in as nuanced a way as they had names and sayings for what to us as outsiders would be only a white featureless expanse. Tarrying in a similar manner with its lack of an Archimedean point, even as Hegel spoke of "tarrying with the

---

[52] G. W. F. Hegel, *Hegel's Philosophy of Mind: Being Part Three of the Encyclopaedia of Philosophical Sciences*, (1830), trans. William Wallace, together with the *Zusätze* in Boumann's text (1845), trans. A. V. Miller, Oxford: Clarendon Press, 1971, § 462, p. 221.

negative,"[53] psychology produces itself and comes into its own via the inseeing that is performed by the "inward externalities" that constitute its own depths even as, making Adams of us all, these appear before it as its topics and subject matters.

But what does it mean for psychology to tarry self-constitutively with its lack of an Archimedean vantage point? Bearing in mind our comparison of this to a peoples' exposure to the so-called barren lands of the arctic, it is enough for our purposes to cite a few passages from Jung. In the context of elucidating the obscure lines of an alchemical text, the great psychologist avers that

> If you will contemplate your lack of fantasy, of inspiration and inner aliveness, which you feel as sheer stagnation and a barren wilderness, and impregnate it with the interest born of alarm at your inner death, then something can take shape in you, for your inner emptiness conceals just as great a fullness if only you will allow it to penetrate into you. If you prove receptive to this 'call of the wild,' the longing for fulfilment will quicken the sterile wilderness of your soul as rain quickens the dry earth.[54]

The second passage has to do with what Jung calls "the highest and most decisive experience of all, which is to be alone with [one's] own self, or whatever else one chooses to call the objectivity of the psyche." About this he incisively declares, "The patient must be alone if he is to find out what it is that supports him when he can no longer support himself. Only this experience can give him an indestructible foundation."[55]

---

[53] Hegel, *The Phenomenology of the Spirit*, § 32, p. 19.

[54] C. G. Jung, *CW* 14 ¶ 190. Helpful as this passage from Jung is for didactic purposes, it falls below the *niveau* of the absolute negative interiority and fecundity we are intent on here. As Wolfgang Giegerich has pointed out to me in a personal email (1 September, 2013): "The only fault I find with Jung's passage is that at the end he says that 'the longing for fulfillment will quicken …': no, not OUR longing and not our LONGING! It is the inseeing into the sterile wilderness itself that brings back life. The wilderness has everything it needs within it." An incisive point.

[55] C.G. Jung, *CW* 12 ¶ 32.

Drawn into our effort to see the Arctic tundra of the ancient Inuit and psychology's lack of an Archimedean point as reflections in the same mirror, these passages from Jung, when freed from their (for our purposes) rather too personalistic focus, bring a reflection of Giegerich's to mind. Also working with the image-concept of "wilderness," Giegerich has discussed how when this is matched by an intentionality of consciousness that is as earnest as its having out-pictured itself to itself as a wilderness is vast, the innermost mystery of that wilderness, the logical negativity of the soul, appears unveiled, in his example, as the goddess Artemis.

> [A]s long as the wilderness appears only as an infinite expanse all around you to which you are exposed, you still see it somehow from outside! Paradoxically, you are not really in it yet, despite having (seemingly) ventured into it and being surrounded by it on all sides. Wilderness as vastness, as contourless wall of otherness, is still an abstraction. It is the simple (undialectical) negation of the positive, domesticated sphere. It is not yet the negative, determinate nought (HEGEL) of the fenced-in realm (negation of the negation). You have positively left the realm of positivity and positively (physically or imaginally) entered the wilderness, but you still behold it from the standpoint of positivity that you brought along with you into the alleged wild. Once you are really in the wild, it also shows itself as Artemis. Artemis is nothing else but the further determination of the notion of 'wilderness,' the revelation of its inner image or mystery.[56]

---

[56] Giegerich, *The Soul's Logical Life*, p. 215. Continuing on page 216 he further explains that "The all-surrounding wilderness, which as such is vast and without contours, is the still positive image of the logical negativity of the soul. Or it is logical negativity still imagined positively. Artemis, by contrast, is the inner secret of this negativity, a secret through which negativity is absolute and not just an ordinary, simple negation: not something like the Nothingness of existentialist thought (the undialectical opposite of Being)." A few lines later he continues, "Artemis is the *negative* experience of the negative, or absolute-negative *Erinnerung* (interiorization) of wilderness. In Artemis, negativity, *if* it has been penetrated deeply enough (i.e., absolutely), reveals itself as being *in itself* not only nothing, a void, contourlessness. This is what makes it absolute (*absolute* negativity)—absolved from the opposition between negativity and positivity." This insightful interpretation of Artemis as the absolute-negative inner secret of the wilderness

Although psychology, as Jung and in his train, Hillman and Giegerich have stressed, has no Archimedean point outside the soul to observe it from objectively, it nevertheless has, as the further determination of its notion "soul," such subjectivity-nuancing and negatively-determining "inward externalities" as "for example a dog as one passes by," a kitten in a coat, and a goddess bathing. Or putting this another way, although there is no one positively-existing vantage point outside the soul upon which a scientist might perch, the dog, the kitten, the goddess, etc., are each singularly expressive of the negative richness (cf., Giegerich's reference to "the *negative, determinate nought*") of the whole soul, even as in Jean Arp's felicitous phrase, "the little holds the big on a leash."[57]

image and of the negativity which the wilderness image only positively figures is all the more illuminating in the context of my discussion of psychology's wilderness-like lack of an Archimedean point. An important implication of this is that the inner secret of the poet's or psychologist's inwardness in the soul may show itself, likewise, in figures as various as Rilke's dog and panther, Melville's Moby Dick, Steinbeck's red pony and the rest.

[57] Cited by Gaston Bachelard in his *The Poetics of Reverie: Childhood, Language, and the Cosmos*, Boston: Beacon Press, 1971, p. 175.

THE INNER INFINITY OF THE ARCHIMEDEANLESS WILD

I said that it is always with a negation that we start—with a stone that is not a stone, a dog that is not a dog, etc. And further to this I spoke variously and in the same breath of the tundra of the ancient Inuit, psychology's lack of an Archimedean point, Jung's advice with respect to exposing oneself to one's apparent emptiness, and Giegerich's interiorizing of the concept of wilderness into itself, i.e., into its further determination as the goddess Artemis. Adding to this, I could just as well have referred to Emerson's reflections on "Nature," in his essay of that title.

Celebrating times spent in meadowlands and forests, Emerson discusses how mindedness, spirit, and truth are speculatively mediated by one's encounters in such seemingly infinite surrounds. "The greatest delight which the fields and woods minister," he writes, "is the suggestion of an occult relation between man and the vegetable. I am not alone and unacknowledged. They nod to me, and I to them. The waving of the boughs in the storm is new to me and old. It takes me by surprise, and yet is not unknown. Its effect is like that of a higher thought or a better emotion coming over me, when I deemed I was thinking justly or doing the right."[58] Surely the Rilke of our passage on inseeing would concur with these reflections. For stamped with what Hegel called the highest inwardness and perfect in the eyes of God, his dog in all likelihood affected him, too, as a higher thought or better emotion coming over him when he thought he was thinking justly or doing right.

But what about the violence of such insight? In "The Epiphany of Artemis" chapter of his *The Soul's Logical Life*, Giegerich discusses how the wilderness that showed itself unveiled in goddess-form as Artemis was, at the same time as it was that, i.e., in another moment

[58] Ralph Waldo Emerson, *Selected Essays*, Larzer Ziff, ed., New York: Penguin Books, 1982, p. 39.

of the soul's syzygial self-relation, the hunter Actaion torn apart by his own dogs.[59] Likewise, in the passage we quoted in which Hegel famously speaks of "tarrying with negative," the life of the spirit is described as "win[ning] its truth only when, in utter dismemberment, it finds itself."[60] Returning from these references to Emerson, we can claim him, too, as an expositor of the insight that nature reflects the spirit in the vast array of its forms. Indeed, as the sub-chapters of his essay, "Language" and "Spirit" show, he was well aware that Nature has been fundamentally sublated. If, however, his meditations in the midst of Nature's forms remain effusive with that sentiment which in the idealist tradition has been criticized under the heading of the Beautiful Soul, this may be because, not being the hunter that the mythical Actaion was, the yield of his nature excursions was limited to lovely edifying insights and did not win through to the vision of ruthless truth unveiled.[61]

Now it is important to keep in mind that our references to "Wilderness," "Nature," and "Tundra," figurative as they are of the absolute inwardness or inner infinity of our having no Archimedean point outside the soul, are fully interchangeable with the forms of spirit and genres of discourse that don these as their garb. The text of a great thinker, for example, though read in an armchair in the comfort of one's home, can, if it is read intensely enough, be as challenging and mysterious as any forest or wilderness area even as (if I may here express myself in the manner of Emerson) a farm can be a church, a mountain range a parliament. And in keeping with this our interest is not in the derivation of one from the other, but in *the logic that pervades both*, which is also to say, with the truths that show themselves in the phenomenon at hand, be this phenomenon

---

[59] Giegerich, *The Soul's Logical Life*, pp. 246-255.

[60] Hegel, *Phenomenology of the Spirit*, § 32, p. 19.

[61] More suspicious than I am of this passage, Giegerich writes me that "… what Emerson says here seems to celebrate immediacy, a naïve simulation of unbornness. No negation, and no inseeing (because he is, or thinks he is, 'in' from the outset." (personal email 1 September 2013).

a creature in the world, a happening in our lives, or a sentence from a book that we simply must underline.

And in this connection, I am put in mind of another passage that I was inspired to thrust my pen at when first I chanced upon it. It is a little text from Meister Eckhart:

> If I were alone in a desert where I was afraid, and if I had a child with me, my fear would disappear and I would be strengthened; so noble, so full of pleasure, and so powerful is life in itself. If I could not keep a child with me and I had at least a live animal with me, I would be comforted. Therefore, let those who bring about great wonders in black books take an animal, perhaps a dog, to help them. The life within the animal will give them strength. Equality gives strength in all things.[62]

The desert that Eckhart refers to in this passage can readily be added to the list I have been keeping in these pages, the one that includes "Wilderness," "Tundra," "Nature" and the inwardness of the soul in itself that psychology knows as its lack of an Archimedean point. In speaking as he does, however, about bringing a child or dog along with him to quell his fear, Eckhart short-changes the true depth of his insight, passing it off as a mere lovely sentiment or piece of advice. This, at any rate, is the objection that comes to light when his text is read and read again in the speculative manner we discussed earlier and which it seems, but only at first glance, not to require.

Simply put, the speculative insight boils down to this: if one were to take a child or a dog along with one, as the mystic recommends, there would be no desert in the first place! And just here in noting this we stumble upon what is contradictory about the advice that is peddled in self-help books. Sensible as such advice may be, it never even sights the psychology of the matter, i.e., the notions that are at stake. But contradicting the contradiction to

---

[62] Cited by Eleanora Woloy, *The Symbol of the Dog in the Human Psyche: A Study of the Human-Dog Bond*, Wilmette: Chiron Publications, 1990, p. 65.

which Eckhart succumbs, let us rise up to the insight that the true child and true dog only appear in the desert as the result of one's tarrying there.

With respect to this essence-producing dialectic any number of examples may be given. The passages I already quoted from Jung about the productiveness of contemplating one's inner emptiness and about the individual's needing to be alone with himself to discover what supports him when he can no longer support himself are of course highly pertinent. Turning now to other examples, I'll confine myself rather arbitrarily to three. In Antoine de Saint-Exupéry's novella, *The Little Prince*, a magical child and a fox (to mention only these) emerge out of the desert in which the aviator's plane is stranded. These figures, it is important to note, have not been brought from outside in the manner advised by Eckhart. Rather, so powerful is the logical life of the soul that they come as the result of his being stranded there. In Wallace Stevens's poem, "Of Mere Being," a "gold-feathered bird" sings "on the edge of space," "beyond the last thought," in "the palm at the end of the mind."[63] In this case, too, the figures referred to are the product and result of the mind's self-othering reflection into itself. And then there is Nietzsche's reference to "... a point in every philosophy when the philosopher's 'conviction' appears on stage—or to use the language of an ancient Mystery: Adventavit asinus, Pulcher et fortissimus [= 'the ass arrived, beautiful and most brave']."[64] In all these passages knowing from within

---

[63] Wallace Stevens, *The Palm at the End of the Mind: Selected Poems and a Play*, Holly Stevens, ed., New York: Vintage Books, 1972, p. 398.

[64] Friedrich Nietzsche, *Beyond Good and Evil,* 15. This line is not as representative as the other examples I have cited of being exposed to the soulful immensity of what is and seeing this from within as an "inward externality." Nietzsche, as we know, railed against truth and so here against the convictions of philosophers. Nevertheless, there is something to be learned from comparing the appearance of the ass he mentions with the move from wilderness to Artemis discussed by Giegerich. Nietzsche, we could say, touches upon the moment when the philosopher's conviction shows its inner contradiction, the moment when Actaion's

displays itself even as, exposed to its own soulful immensity, mindedness, consciousness or "the soul" out-pictures itself to itself in the form of the aforementioned "inward externalities." And here, again, let us recall Giegerich's insight about how the wilderness when seen from within shows itself as Artemis. In much the same way (and yet in each instance differently!) Saint-Exupéry's little prince and fox, Rilke's dog and panther, Jung's pig, Nietzsche's donkey, and Stevens's palm tree and golden bird only come into being in the first place as the sublation of their environs and context, which is also to say, as the mutually mediating entirety of the *mise-en-scène* that they proto-conceptually express in their allegorical and pars pro toto manner.

Taking these reflections a little further we can say that like the stone that is not a stone, so the dog that is not dog, along with all the other figures that could be mentioned in this regard,[65] are not what they immediately seem to be. Rather, sublated from the outset, the result to begin with (!) of all that they are not, they are thoughts that have been given "the form of objectivity, of being distinct from our inwardness," as we already heard from Hegel. And here at this juncture I might as well claim another passage from Hegel for our PDI discourse. In a related context, the great philosopher states,

> *To sublate* and the *sublated* (that which exists ideally as a moment), constitute one of the most important notions in philosophy. It is a fundamental determination which repeatedly occurs throughout the whole of philosophy, the meaning of which is to be clearly grasped and especially distinguished from *nothing*. What is sublated is not thereby reduced to nothing. Nothing is *immediate*; what is sublated, on the other hand, is the result of *mediation*; it is

---

dogs turn upon him. That the contradiction of a philosopher's conviction, which has the explicitly conceptual form of an argument or judgment, appears as an imaginal form, shows that it was not as fully and successfully the concept it thought itself to be.

[65] Any compelling phenomenon or subject matter could be mentioned. "Everything is not itself," said Rilke in the fourth of his *Duino Elegies*.

a nonbeing but as a *result* which had its origin in a being. It still has, therefore, *in itself* the *determinateness from which it originates.*"[66]

In this passage the statement "Nothing is immediate" corresponds in imaginal terms to the empty vastness of "Wilderness," "Desert," "Tundra," etc. Though not really and truly nothing,[67] for after all these various settings do have a ground in the determinateness of actual being, the way they can be drawn upon to represent nothing gives rise to a nonbeing, or in other words, to thinking, cognition, spirit and thought. And this thinking, cognition, spirit and thought, it is important to stress, is the determinate result of the negativity that the all-surrounding "Wilderness," "Desert," and "Tundra," etc., sensually convey through their having been further negated and further realized.

* * *

We began with Rilke's remarks about an aspect of his poetic sensibility. "Can you imagine with me," he exuberantly exclaims in a letter to a friend, "how glorious it is to insee ...." Rigorously conceived, the thought that such inseeing describes is a matter of an essence-producing mindedness. And it is this, moreover, even when, as our poet offers, the first immediacy of such mindedness is "a dog as one passes by."—Or so I aver our efforts to interiorize Rilke's vision of interiority into itself permit us to conclude.

Addressing himself to the same topic, but of course without reference to the author and text that have concerned us in these pages, Giegerich has described such insight as involving the *a*

---

[66] This passage is generally referred to as Hegel's "Speculative Remark," as it can be found in the section with that subtitle that Hegel added to the 2nd edition of *The Science of Logic.*

[67] As Hegel has pointed out, "nothing" or "non-being" cannot be thought apart from its opposite, "something" or "being," and this being so the mind is conducted of its own accord to the sublated unity of this identity and difference, the concept "becoming."

posteriori cognition of the *a priori* spirit as which the phenomenon-at-hand exists—or again, as a matter of psychological phenomena producing their own *a priori* as their *a posteriori* result.[68] Reflecting upon this in terms that are fully compatible with what I said above about the recursive, subject-seconding character of the predicate in speculative sentences, he states: "For a true psychology, the *a priori* has to be absolutely-negatively interiorized, involuted, into its other, the *a posteriori*, the actual event of the deed, so as to close the uroboric circle and give to 'making' its full meaning. The prior, the origin, is a result of, and later than, what is originated by it."[69]

In our text from Rilke the inseeing that is described involves a similar dialectic. It is only *a posteriori*-ly, that is, only after the dog is finished, so to speak, that the *a priori*, God, climbs into it, or better, radiates out from it. Or expressing this again in terms of what we learned about the speculative sentence, it is only after we have seen the dog "… under the influence of its first embarrassments and inspirations…" that we know what or who the "God" in Rilke's text (and in a sentence such as "God created the dog") is in the first place.

Now, of course, the poet is not referring to God per se. It is his acuity as a poet in what he calls his "timeless moments of divine inseeing" that he is concerned with. And further to this, we can liken inseeing to what the Bible calls "discriminating the spirits." Contrary, however, to the Apostle's admonishment that "we test the spirits to see whether they are from God" (1 John 4:1), psychology produces itself and comes into its own via the religion-sublating insight that there are not first entity-like spirits, which we the faithful then discriminate between, but rather and in the manner of the *a posteriori*-ly discriminated *a priori* discussed by Giegerich, spirits that are produced, gods that are conceived, by the discriminating, name-giving power of

---

[68] Wolfgang Giegerich, *Soul-Violence, CEP,* vol. III, pp. 32, 213. Also his *What Is Soul?*, pp, 37, 41. 58, 306.

[69] Giegerich, *Soul-Violence, CEP*, vol. III, p. 32.

mind. "There are many souls," writes Nietzsche, "that one will never uncover, unless one invents them first."[70]

Just as a wine connoisseur may be able name a particular wine's year of vintage and even the field where its grapes were gown, perhaps there is some literary connoisseur who can name the park in Berlin or Paris where Rilke beheld the dog that he writes of in his text, distinguishing in the same breath the God-filled spirit of such an occasion from the epiphanies of divine inseeing that have been variously inspired by the tundra of the Inuit, the desert of Saint-Exupéry's fiction, and the trackless forest in which the mythical Actaion was torn apart by his hounds after coming upon the goddess bathing. Not that we want to know the dates and the places. Our interest, rather, is in how the wine in the one case and the literary specimen in the other epitomize, essentialize, and exemplify the logic that pervades both. Externally conceived as dateable periods and intersecting lines of longitude and latitude, time and place are soul-less abstractions. Leaving such abstract conceptions behind, even as we have left thinking it terms of an Archimedean vantage point behind, our interest is wholly invested in what now at the end of this essay may variously be called "the negative determinate naught," "inward externality," and "absolute negative interiorization," the only proviso to this being that with these terms we do not merely propose a new set of abstractions, but are referring to those phenomena appearing in front consciousness that want, as it were, to become the new form of consciousness-at-large,[71] in Hegel's famous line, to the Owl of Minerva that only flies at dusk,[72] in Rilke's example, to "a dog as one passes by."

---

[70] Friedrich Nietzsche, *Thus Spoke Zarathustra*, trans. R. J. Hollingdale, Harmondsworth: Penguin Books, 1969, p. 69.

[71] Again, see Giegerich, "Is the Soul 'Deep?'," *CEP*, vol. IV, p. 149: "…what at first appears as a content [or object] of consciousness is in truth the seed of what wants to become a new form of consciousness at large."

[72] G. W. F. Hegel, *Hegel's Philosophy of Right*, trans. T. M. Knox, London: Oxford University Press, 1967, p. 13.

THE DOG THAT IS NOT A DOG

> … [L]et those who bring about great wonders in black books take an animal, perhaps a dog, to help them. The life within the animal will give them strength. …[1]
>
> —Meister Eckhart

IN HIS ESSAY, "The absolute that is not absolute: an alchemical reflection on the caput mortuum, the dark other of logical light,"[2] Stanton Marlan critically engages with Wolfgang Giegerich's contribution to Jungian psychology, but this in a manner that mischaracterizes the school of Jungian psychology that stems from this contribution—Psychology as the Discipline of Interiority (hereafter, PDI[3]). I limit myself to two examples of such mischaracterization: his claim that PDI has "no dog in the fight"[4] and his claim that PDI is "too pure [a psychology] to treat ordinary human beings in the consulting room."[5]These are serious charges. All the more so, coming as they do from PDI's most informed and respected critic. According to its conception of itself, PDI is a mode

---

[1] Cited by Eleanora Woloy, *The Symbol of the Dog in the Human Psyche: A Study of the Human-Dog Bond.* Wilmette: Chiron Publications, 1990, p. 65.

[2] Stanton Marlan, "The absolute that is not absolute: an alchemical reflection on the caput mortuum, the dark other of logical light," *International Journal of Jungian Studies*, DOI: 10.1080/19409052.2016.1237372. This paper was first given as a talk at The Third International Conference for the International Society for Psychology as the Discipline of Interiority, May 12-14, 2016, Serra Retreat Center, Malibu California.

[3] I have resorted to the use of this acronym for the sake of convenience. Its use, however, comes at the cost of implying a school of psychology alongside of others, when my intention is actually not that of contributing to one particular school of psychology in preference to some other school, but of advancing to a truly *psychological* psychology.

[4] Marlan, *op. cit.,* p. 5.

[5] Marlan, *op. cit.*, p. 12.

of psychological thinking that puts itself, its very definition of soul, at stake on each interpretive occasion. Whatever its topics or subject matters may be, its view of itself is that it only comes into its own via a self-othering mode of cognition that defines and redefines itself, or better, the concept it exists as, by the reflection of the phenomena commanding its attention more deeply into themselves. It is a matter, if I may put it this way, of a "bone of my bone, flesh of my flesh" dialectic.[6] Just as Adam, the speaker of these words, came to know the woman, Eve, who had been fashioned for him out of one of his own ribs, so the subject side of the ordinarily prevailing difference of consciousness comes to know itself via a soul-seconding encounter with what it meets with on the object side of that difference. And here I am prompted to recall a statement of Giegerich's: "[P]sychology begins where any phenomenon (whether physical or mental, 'real' or fantasy image) is interiorized absolute-negatively into itself, and I find myself in its internal infinity. This is what it takes; psychology cannot be had for less."[7]—Now if this psychological approach is not to have "a dog in the fight," I must confess myself bewildered as to what that phrase could mean. And the same bewilderment comes over me with respect to Marlan's characterizing of PDI as "too pure [a psychology] to treat ordinary human beings in the consulting room." Both Giegerich and myself are practicing analysts. For Marlan to lay such a charge at our door can only mean that he does not think that we really practice in the PDI vein that we represent and write about!

---

[6] My putting it this way follows Hegel, who wrote (with Genesis, ii, 23 in mind): "Just as Adam said to Eve: 'Thou art flesh of my flesh and bone of my bone,' so mind says 'This is mind of my mind and its foreign character has disappeared.'" G.W. F. Hegel, *Philosophy of Right*, trans. T. M. Knox, London: Oxford University Press, 1967, p. 226.

[7] Giegerich, "Is the Soul 'Deep'?—Entering and Following the Logical Movement of Heraclitus' 'Fragment 45'," *Spring 64: A Journal of Archetype and Culture*, Fall & Winter, 1998, p. 31. Also, in *CEP*, vol. IV, pp. 161-162.

In the pages that follow I will address these criticisms of Marlan's as two sides of the same coin. But before I get to that I want briefly to discuss the wider context within which they have arisen. Marlan's paper is the latest of a volley of exchanges between him and Giegerich in which the differences between them are discussed in relation to differences between the philosophies of Kant and Hegel.[8] No doubt this is an important, if somewhat arcane, topic. Not only Marlan and Giegerich, but a number of Jungian authors have written about these great philosophers.[9] The only problem that this literature poses is that there are as many Kants and as many Hegels as there are writers to write about them. Not that this issue is exclusive to Jung and Jungians. Even dedicated scholars of Kant disagree about "what Kant really meant,"[10] and the same can be said of Hegel scholars

[8] Stanton Marlan's, "From the Black Sun to the Philosophers' Stone," in: *Spring 74*, pp. 1-30, is responded to by Wolfgang Giegerich in his "'The unassimilable Remnant': What is at Stake? A Dispute with Stan Marlan," which appeared in *Archetypal Psychologies. Reflections in Honor of James Hillman*, New Orleans: Spring Journal Books, 2008, pp. 193-223. There then followed two further articles by Marlan: his "The psychologist that is not a psychologist: a deconstructive reading of Wolfgang Giegerich's idea of psychology proper," *Journal of Analytical Psychology*, vol. 61, no. 2, April 2016, pp. 223-238 and his "The absolute that is not absolute: an alchemical reflection on the caput mortuum, the dark other of logical light," *International Journal of Jungian Studies*, DOI: 10.1080/19409052.2016.1237372.

[9] Stephanie de Voogd, "C. G. Jung: Psychologist of the Future 'Philosopher' of the Past," *Spring* 1977, pp. 175-182; Stephanie de Voogd, "Fantasy versus Fiction: Jung's Kantianism Appraised," in R. K. Papadopoulos and G. S. Saayman, eds., *Jung in Modern Perspective* (London: Wildwood House, 1984), pp. 204-28; Barbara Eckman, "Jung, Hegel, and the Subjective Universe," *Spring* 1986, pp. 88-99; Wolfgang Giegerich, "The Rescue of the World: Jung, Hegel and the Subjective Universe," *Spring* 1987, pp. 107-114; Joseph F. Rychlak, "Jung as Dialectician and Teleologist," in *op. cit.*, *Jung in Modern Perspective*, pp. 34-53; Hester Solomon, "The Transcendent Function and Hegel's Dialectical Vision," *Journal of Analytical Psychology*, 39, (1994): 77-100; Wolfgang Giegerich, David L. Miller, Greg Mogenson, *Dialectics & Analytical Psychology: The El Capitan Canyon Seminar*, New Orleans: Spring Journal Books, 2005; Wolfgang Giegerich, "Jung's Betrayal of His Truth. The Adoption of a Kant-Based Empiricism and the Rejection of Hegel's Speculative Thought," and "'Jung and Hegel' Revisited. Or: The Seelenproblem of Modern Man and the 'Doubt-that-has-killed-it'," both in *CEP*, vol. VI, chapters 6 and 7, respectively.

with respect to Hegel. Little wonder then that when our disputes in psychology draw upon these figures even those of us who have done our philosophy homework may be left to wonder what is really being argued, really being said. Fortunately, however, for my purposes here, it will not be necessary for us to be drawn into such disputes. It will be enough to examine what Marlan's Kant and Hegel authorize and inspire him to additionally say in his essay.[11]

Turning to this now, the first thing to be said is that Marlan's text is chock-full of phrases that are representative of his take on these philosophers. For example, further to Kant's epistemologically contrite distinction between phenomena as they appear to us and the unknowable noumenon or "thing in itself," he speaks of the importance of our recognizing "an unassimilable remainder that sets a limit to the [Hegelian] idea that all otherness ultimately is for consciousness."[12] "[T]here always remains," he goes on to explain, "a dark remnant in the [alchemical] retort after distillation. It remains other and opaque to consciousness and maintains its resistance to being accounted for by a movement in a dialectic intending to make it serve as a mark of differentiation of a higher sublation."[13] Of course, the last of these words are an allusion to Hegel and Giegerich. "Throughout his thought," writes Marlan, "Hegel and Giegerich after him defend a view intended to overcome difference through a speculative (if differentiated) unity."[14] To their own satisfaction, if not to Marlan's, Hegel and Giegerich have negated the negation that philosophy via the work of Kant challenged

---

[10] With this wording I allude to the book by E. A. Bennet, *What Jung Really Said*, New York: Schocken Books, 1967.

[11] My emphasis here might be described as one of *lebensphilosophie*, this in the sense of how a particular philosophy, psychology, or theoretical stance handles life.

[12] Marlan, "The absolute that is not absolute," p. 2.

[13] *Ibid.*, p. 7.

[14] *Ibid.*, p. 5.

itself with, the upshot of this being that there is in their view no subject matter from which the speculative mind must turn back, no other which it cannot be at home in (or redefinitionally come home to itself through), no unassimilable remainder or remnant. But here is the rub. Like that just mentioned remainder or remnant which he insists upon, Marlan is unconvinced. Despite his own having witnessed in Giegerich's writings such PDI-constituting feats of interpretation beyond Kantian limits as "leaping into stone walls, climbing glass mountains, and finding truth by chasing a naked goddess,"[15] he continues to insist upon the untransformable dross of the alchemists. "My work," he steadfastly reiterates, "began with the recognition that the image of the black sun resisted conscious assimilation—that it would not yield or be incorporated, did not dissolve, go away, go under, get lifted up, but rather remained to challenge one's psychological narcissism to the core, [with] experiences of brokenness, incision, wound, castration, cut[,] negation, and with an ultimate 'no' to consciousness."[16]

There is more to be highlighted with respect to what Marlan's take on Kant and Hegel authorizes and inspires him to additionally—and uniquely—say in his essay. Further to what was shown of this in the previous paragraph, I find especially noteworthy his poignant account of the passing away of his beloved dog, Curtis. It is perhaps surprising, this turn in his argument. Following upon some four and a half pages in which his philosophical differences with Giegerich are discussed, he suddenly changes his tone and plunges into a personal story of his grief and loss:

> I recently had to euthanize Curtis, a deeply loved companion over many years. I held out doing so until his suffering was undeniable and I felt it cruel to hold onto him for my sake. In my last hours with Curt, I lay with him in his bed, held him as my grief

[15] Marlan, "The absolute that is not absolute," p. 3.

[16] *Ibid.*, p. 6.

> deepened. His breath was hard and obstructed, and he had lost the use of his legs. I looked into his eyes as if hoping for an acknowledgment of what was to come. I inhaled his outward breath and he inhaled mine. This went on for some time and at one moment he licked my face and this gave me the capacity to move forward. The next morning, Curt was euthanized. I held him as the needle pinched him in the back of the neck and he slowly drifted away from his pain in a deep relaxation, release and the oblivion of sleep. Then, the injection of chemicals followed that would transform him from living animation to a lifeless form. I continue to grieve Curtis, who was cremated, and whose remains sit at home and continue to fill me with a mixture of grief, love, and wonder.[17]

Marlan's readers, no doubt, will easily empathize with the experience he describes. Some may even be reminded of similar experiences from their own lives. I know I was. But as serious-minded readers of psychology we must also discern the argumentative purpose of Marlan's referring to his dog's demise. What does his dog story have to do with the philosophical differences between Kant and Hegel? And what role does it play in his psychological dispute with Giegerich and PDI? Before citing what Marlan goes on to say about these matters, I want quickly to suggest a few preliminary answers of my own (while keeping back my ultimate answer until later in this essay). In the abstract given at the top of his article, Marlan states that in contrast to Giegerich and PDI, his own psychological position "resists the successionist ideas of a post-Jungian, trans-human perspective and asserts the notion of an unassimilable and unsurmountable 'not'."[18] Adding on, he states further to this that he will be revisioning the traditional divide between the philosophers, Kant and Hegel, by "taking the 'thing-in-itself' as truly other than existing only for consciousness and [on this basis] arguing against [Giegerich's] privileging the *unity* of unity and difference."[19] Now it is important

[17] Marlan, "The absolute that is not absolute," p. 5.
[18] *Ibid.*, p. 1.

to realize that Marlan's account of the grief he feels over the passing of his dog is in keeping with this theoretical aim. His beloved Curtis, whose loss he feels so deeply, has in its pedigree something of Kant's *noumenon,* the unknowable thing-it-itself. Just as Kant posited an unknowable thing-in-itself that is truly other than the phenomena we experience (and presumably the untouchable, unthinkable, unknowable touchstone of their mystery), so Marlan insists upon the unassimilable autonomy, otherness, and mystery character of Curtis beyond even the rich phenomenology of their friendship through the years as dog and master, and now into death. Why, it can even be said that Curtis is a most worthy mascot within the pages of an article in which his master "entertains alchemical ideas of a residue, a *caput mortuum*, and an archetypally cumbersome object, a real limit, which remains and unhinges the elevating process of spirit on its path to return into itself in absolute interiority."[20] For that, presumably, is what he was and is and why his master loves him so. And it is also why, in contradistinction to the claim of what he calls Giegerich's "pure psychology" to have surpassed Kant's and Jung's distinction between phenomenon and noumenon, that Marlan proudly describes his own approach to psychology as being "a darker art" and "mongrel mix."[21]

But there is more to be said about this. Another argumentative purpose of Marlan's dog story has to do with the human sentiment

---

[19] Handing PDI the dirty end of the stick, Marlan's seemingly modest and epistemologically circumspect idea of "taking the 'thing-in-itself' as truly other than existing only for consciousness" implies by contrast that PDI's stance with respect to the phenomena it deals with is narcissistic, solipsistic. Instead of existing in and for itself, the phenomena it takes up as its prime matter exist only for consciousness. But PDI does not identify with consciousness in this monopolizing way. Its position, rather, is that its other is also a subject, a subject, moreover, that being what it is, uroborically mediates the redefinition of the arbitrarily first-mentioned subject, being at the same time its other.

[20] Marlan, "The absolute that is not absolute," p. 1.

[21] *Ibid.*, p. 12.

it conveys. This, evidently, is intended by its author as a heartwarmingly soulful showing up of what he believes to be lacking in PDI. As was mentioned at the outset, Marlan regards PDI as being "too pure [a psychology] to treat ordinary human beings in the consulting room."[22] In keeping with this he asserts in another statement that "Giegerich leans too far in the direction of overcoming and going beyond the 'human, all-to-human' person" and attributes this fault to his having "defin[ed] psychology proper in such a way as to create a divide, a radical cut, that has led to an imbalance between his vision of psychology and the everyday life of our empirical experience."[23] Marlan's story of the passing of his beloved Curtis, by contrast, aims to show his own psychological approach to be in complete rapport with the empirical human experience of everyday life. But is it truly the case that PDI is helpless before such everyday life experience? Really so that it cannot deal with ordinary human beings in the consulting room? I shall be returning to this topic in a moment, by means of the case example Marlan makes of himself in his article. But before turning to this let us briefly examine his further remarks about the loss of his dog and about what this experience means for psychology in the context of his dispute with Giegerich and PDI.

---

[22] Marlan, "The absolute that is not absolute," p. 12.

[23] *Ibid.*, p. 12. What Marlan here characterizes as "a cut, a radical divide" is a reference to Giegerich's concept of the psychological difference, but one that mischaracterizes this concept. While it is true that with this concept Giegerich releases the psychological mind from the kinds of psychic phenomena other psychologies base their insights on, this is a methodological move to establish an analytical attitude that is able to discern "the soul" of such phenomena. As Giegerich writes: "For a true psychology, only the soul, which is certainly undemonstrable, merely 'metaphorical' and for this reason a seeming nothing, can be the 'substrate' and subject of the phenomena. The human being is then their object; he or she is nothing but the place where soul shows itself, just like the world is the place where man shows himself and becomes active. We therefore must shift our standpoint away from 'the human person' to the 'soul.' (N.B.: I am talking of a shift of *our standpoint, perspective, or of the idea in terms of which* we study, just as before the concrete experience of individuals and peoples.) "The Present as Dimension of the Soul. 'Actual Conflict' and Archetypal Psychology," *CEP.,* Vol. I, p. 115.

Following immediately upon his moving account of having had to euthanize Curtis, Marlan continues:

> Curt remains for me something more than a conceptual, noetic, linguistic dog. He was my friend, actual, independent, objective and deeply natural. I know that the noetic has its objectivity too and I do believe there is an intrinsic soul-bond with Curtis. Something noetic, sublated from the beginning, but my relationship to him also leads me back to Jacobi's early criticism of Fichte's and Hegel's idealism. For Hegel and Giegerich, the subject's realization of its final identity is with what seemed other to it. The object world turns out to be thinking itself, where substance is subject and one meets oneself beyond the vale. Yet for me, this formulation does not fully satisfy my relationship with Curtis and I hold with Jacobi that what really matters lies both before and outside an idealistic reduction to knowledge.[24]

Continuing his criticism in the next paragraph, Marlan sends his theory-asserting dog deeper into the fight:

> From the place of Giegerich's uroboric understanding of psyche, otherness remains internal to itself, logically not inner or outer, everything becomes mental and noetic. There is no subject-object. The traditional divide is overcome. No more tension between inner and outer. Spatial relations are dissolved. Psyche becomes totally autonomous, thinking itself essential truth in an act of self-knowing—psychic reality gone wild—on steroids! The 'actual' other is dismissed and my dog becomes my mind and my mind my dog. This view does not satisfy me, nor account for the reality of my relation to Curtis.[25]

Marlan's position is clear. His dog transcends his apperception of him. Why, it could even be said that he is as extra-psychic as the thing-in-itself is extra-phenomenal—an absolute that *is* absolute (in some pre-Hegelian and abstract sense). In contrast to PDI's

---

[24] Marlan, "The absolute that is not absolute," p. 5-6.

[25] *Ibid.*, p. 6.

claim to a speculative knowledge that cancels the subject-here/object-there difference of consciousness within the more comprehensive concepts of itself that consciousness ever and again achieves thereby, Curtis is mysteriously, unknowably, himself, and this, moreover, in a way that not only mediates the so-called "unassimilable remainder," but bodies it forth "as man's best friend." The only thing that needs additionally to be added is that Marlan's references to a "conceptual, noetic, linguistic dog" derive from and critically refer back to the previous article of mine having to do with the poet Rilke's contemplation of a dog via an imaginative mode of cognition that he called "inseeing."[26] Appreciative of this article for what it shows with respect to PDI's methodology of absolute-negative interiorization, Marlan clearly is also appreciative of the opportunity it provides to critique that methodology via his story of Curtis's death. It is only fitting then, given Marlan's having been prompted to write of his real and actual dog by what I wrote about "a dog that is not a dog," that it should now be my task to analyze the sublatedness of Curtis as a figure in his dispute with PDI.

For simplicity's sake, I begin with a banality. It is routinely the case in psychotherapy that insights arise when the topics presented and facts discussed are suspected of having an additional meaning or second sense which is unconscious to the patient. Every day in our practices we hear about all manner of events and experiences, attending to these with empathy, fellow-feeling, and sympathetic concern. Occasionally, however, it also happens that these events and experiences impart a different meaning, something other than and seemingly alien to the one they had literally seemed to have. As Jung puts it in an oft-quoted passage, "… behind the impressions of the daily life—behind the scenes—another picture looms up, covered by a thin veil of facts."[27]

---

[26] See the Acknowledgments page above for more information.

Is this not also the case with Marlan's article? Does another picture not loom up in its pages? As I have already pointed out, in the midst of a high-level theoretical dispute touching upon how differences between the philosophies of Kant and Hegel have put two schools of Jungian psychology at loggerheads with each other, Marlan all of a sudden launches into the story of his having held his beloved dog while it was being euthanized! On the one hand, what we have here can readily be taken up as belonging to "the everyday life of our empirical experience." A psychologist, who in addition to being a psychologist is also an ordinary pet owner, suffers grief after putting his pet down. On the other hand, this scene of life may also be taken as an uncanny image of the psychologist Marlan's dispute with Giegerich and PDI—his psychology at a theoretical level seen from within.

So we are faced, as is usually the case, with a two-fold interpretive challenge. In keeping with this, a convention of PDI holds that the psychological difference (between the psychic and the psychological) runs through the consulting room. The therapist, it follows, must be capable of both. He must be able to empathize with the patient's personal feelings and life situation while at the same time being open to the other picture that may loom up while he is doing so. And it is the same, I maintain, with respect to Marlan's article. We must both empathize with his story about the death of Curtis and be able to see through to the logical shift in the soul's life that this story unwittingly reflects and points to at the theoretical level.

Now with this in mind, let us press on. Early in his paper, Marlan establishes the ground for the just-mentioned logical shift and theoretical change that his dog story at one and the same time both accomplishes and resists. "I would like to begin," he trenchantly declares, "with Dr. Giegerich's question, what is at stake in [Marlan's] notion of an unassimilable remnant?" Immediately answering, Marlan

---

[27] C. G. Jung, *The Visions Seminars*, Book One, Zürich: Spring Publications, 1976, p. 8.

states that "One thing that is at stake is [Giegerich's] view of 'psychology proper'." Following this he then asks, "How or to what extent does Giegerich's work surpass Jung's or Hillman's?"[28] The reference here is to "Giegerich [having] argue[d] vigorously to demonstrate and to prove that his view of psychology is superior, a successionist move beyond Jung and Hillman."[29]

So there we have it! Reading and re-reading Marlan's article, it is when I come upon these sentences that "the other picture looms up" and I find that his story about the death of his dog outside of his text (but told about within it!) gives way to the death of "that dog that is not a dog," the sublated Curtis that figures in his article. For surely it is not only pet dogs that can die and be deeply grieved, but pet-theories and pet-theorists, too. But let me spell this out.

PDI—*Marlan's* PDI!—has had a dog in the fight. And this dog appearing in his text is dead. Does this not mean that something has gone under, died, even had to be euthanized, in Marlan's own theoretical position? We have to realize (as Marlan well knows in other contexts) that there is no referent outside the text, no concept or thing transcendent to it. The Curtis of his text belongs to and is a product of his text. As Hillman would have expressed it, in Marlan's article we have an image *as* Curtis, not an image *of* him.[30] In contrast to the actual dog that might have fetched a stick for its master in a park, or greeted a patient with him at his office door, the dog in Marlan's text lives, moves, and has its being—or rather the negative of these, is euthanized, dies and expires—amongst references to Kant, Hegel, Jacobi, Jung, Hillman, Giegerich and myself. A "mongrel mix," indeed, though not of the canine species!

---

[28] Marlan, "The absolute that is not absolute," p. 6.

[29] *Ibid.*, p. 2.

[30] See James Hillman, "Further Notes on Images," *Spring 1978*, p. 173. The image of Curtis being euthanized might also put us in mind of Hillman's notion of what he calls "pathologizing" and his notion of an "Underworld perspective" which reflects the soul's relation with death.

Above I said that I could readily empathize with Marlan's grief over the loss of his dog, having been a dog-owner myself. But turning now from the psychic to the psychological side of the psychological difference, I would also like to say that I have as much compassion and fellow-feeling for the comparable loss (and negative boon!) that is brought about, not by a needle injecting chemicals into the neck of a dog that is being euthanized, but by the "with Jung, against Jung, beyond Jung" dialectic through which what Jung once called "my critical psychology"[31] plumbs and unfolds the depths of its notion through the thinking of its successor analysts—Hillman, Giegerich, Marlan, et., al. And here, as I attempt to convey this other loss that may be detected by seeing-through the literal one, I am prompted to recall an exchange I had with Giegerich some years prior to my becoming the editor of his *Collected English Papers.* In a personal email I wrote to him as follows:

> I hope that you will recognize that my occasional quarrelsomeness is part of working this [my disillusionment with some of Jung's ideas] through. There is a motto: "Don't throw out your antiques before you know what they are worth." I'm sure my encounter with your thought will require me to throw out some antiques. I can't do it, though—just like that!—but only laboriously.[32]

A few days later, I received a reply:

> ... I can sympathize very much with what you say and with the emotional difficulties that what I write create, with the need to rescue the inner core of Jung's project, etc.—because this is how I felt earlier too. It has been a long way for me to slowly understand what personal 'ideological' needs of mine Jung's psychology satisfied for me, and my critique of 'Jung' is thus also

[31] C. G. Jung, *Letters*, vol. 2, G. Adler, ed., Princeton: Princeton University Press, 1975.

[32] Personal email, October 16, 2000.

> a cutting into my own flesh to some extent. But I think it was worth it.
>
> As to: Don't throw out your antiques before you know what they are worth, I agree, but I would want to add an additional idea. In my youth I once read [in] a book a sentence which stayed with me: One must possess money in order to be able to have contempt for it. Now here, in the matter of Jung, it is not a question of having contempt at all. But what is important in this sentence for me is the idea that before one can throw out any antiques, one has to have really owned them. And this is why I appreciate you defending Jung. Any premature critiquing would be a mistake.
>
> And this leads me to a second addition. Maybe one can find out the worth of one's antiques only AFTER one has thrown them out. Because only then does one have the distance necessary to critically appreciate them, rather than being sort of infatuated with them.[33]

Throwing out one's antiques, cutting into one's own flesh, euthanizing a beloved pet—reminded by these images of Marlan's having charged PDI with being "too pure [a psychology] to treat ordinary human beings in the consulting room," I would now like to ask: is this email exchange between Giegerich and myself really so different from the exchanges that happen in consulting rooms everywhere? On the one hand, there is the analyst's sympathetic understanding of the emotional difficulties that a situation involves, and further to this, his understanding of the personal ideological needs that are no longer satisfied by the definition of the soul that had previously prevailed. On the other hand, the words and images which have been utilized to present these concerns are reflected into themselves such that the prose of the ego (speaking only of its ordinary needs, attachments, and concerns) gives way to the poetry of the soul (i.e., to its speaking re-definitionally about itself).

---

[33] Personal email, October 20, 2000.

It is important to stress that I am not arguing that the negation of the theoretical contributions of Jung and Hillman, which Marlan's story of his dog's death can be seen-through to reflect, is brought about by Giegerich and PDI having somehow shown Marlan up or bettered him in the course of their ongoing dispute. For strictly speaking, the negation that PDI is at once both about and constituted by is nothing so external as that. On the contrary, as Giegerich has pointed out in an earlier reply to Marlan (which was included by Marlan in a *festschrift* for Hillman volume that he edited![34]), in the psychological (as distinct from psychic) sense, negation is always a matter of a sublation-mediating self-negation. "It is the realization that the matter has all along not been what it had seemed to be. And this is at once the (first immediacy of the) recognition of the new form of the matter."[35]

It should now be clear, the reason that I referred a few paragraphs back to "*Marlan's* PDI." It is his own implicit PDI, which he represents to himself in his story of his having had to euthanize his dog, that negates and sublates his Jung and Hillman, not Giegerich's or my explicit PDI.[36] And here I am prompted to

---

[34] Stanton Marlan, ed., *Archetypal Psychologies: Reflections in Honor of James Hillman*, New Orleans: Spring Journal Books, 2008.

[35] Wolfgang Giegerich, "'The Unassimilable Remnant'—What Is at Stake?," in ibid., p. 219. Also, in *CEP*, vol. IV, p. 427.

[36] PDI produces itself and proceeds by means of a "with psychology, against psychology, the more truly to become psychology (i.e., *psychological* psychology)" dialectic. Looking back, it may be argued that it was by pursuing such a dialectic that the Freudian Jung sublated his apprenticeship to Freud to produce his successor psychology. "In retrospect," he writes in *MDR*, p. 168, "I can say that I alone logically pursued the two problems which most interested Freud: the problem of 'archaic vestiges,' and that of sexuality." In our present context it is important to highlight the psychic pain that such transformations of the transference may involve. The "against psychology" moment of the dialectic tends to be as emotionally difficult as it is theoretically necessary, as my earlier references to throwing out antiques, cutting into one's own flesh, and euthanizing a beloved dog may serve to convey. And in this connection we may think of the dream Jung reports of his having to kill the mythical hero Siegfried: "After the deed I felt an overpowering compassion, as though I myself had been shot: a sign of my secret identity with Siegfried, as well as of the grief a man feels when he is forced to

recall a passage from the Hegel scholar, John N. Findlay: "The action of thought is to *negate* the basis from which it starts, to show it up as not being self-subsistent, and so to have in it a springboard from which it can ascend to what is truly self-subsistent and self-explanatory."[37]

It is a moving and impressive feat. I cannot think of another critic of Giegerich and PDI who even comes close to having achieved it. Those he mentions, Saban[38] and McGrath[39] (and there are more besides these[40]), do not in their contributions to this dispute have command of even enough curiosity to kill a cat, let alone of enough "intentionality toward the other"[41] to euthanize a dearly loved dog! But Marlan's dog does die, not only the one he knew in life, but the one he discusses in his text. In his grief, Marlan lies strewn with him in a dismembered embrace of love, Curtis and he inhaling and exhaling each other's last breaths. He is like Actaion torn apart by his own hounds. I am referring, of

---

sacrifice his ideal and his conscious attitudes" (*MDR*, p. 180). And much the same for the "with Jung, against Jung, the more truly to become Jungian" dialectic suffered by all successor analysts who would come into their own.

37. John N. Findlay, "Foreword," In G. W. F. Hegel, *Hegel's Logic: Being Part One of the Encyclopedia of Philosophical Sciences*, trans. William Wallace, Oxford: Clarendon Press, 1975, pp. v-xxvii.

38 Mark Saban, "Another serious misunderstanding: Jung, Giegerich and a premature requiem," *Journal of Analytical Psychology*, 2015, 60, 1, 94-113, which was responded to by Giegerich in his "Two Jungs. Apropos a paper by Mark Saban," *Journal of Analytical Psychology*, 2015, vol. 60, no. 3, pp. 303-315.

39 Sean McGrath, "The question concerning metaphysics: A Schellingian intervention in analytical psychology," *International Journal of Jungian Studies*, 2014, vol. 6, no. 1, 23-51, http:/10.1080/19409052.2013.795183. Responded to by Giegerich in his "Jungian psychology as metaphysics? A response to Sean McGrath," *International Journal of Jungian Studies*, 2014, DOI: 10.1080/19409052.2014.954438.

40 Sheila Grimaldi-Craig (a pseudonym!), "Wolfgang's world," *Spring 64: A Journal of Archetype and Culture,* Fall & Winter, 1998, pp. 185-198; Michael Vannoy Adams, "The Naked & the Veiled: Soul, Logic and Absolute Truth," *The Round Table Review*, March/April 1999, pp. 14-17; Robert Romanyshyn, "Who is Wolfgang Giegerich?" *Spring 84*, Fall 2010, pp. 273-310; Glen Slater, "No as if, no between: the Giegerich inversion of mind and soul," *ibid.*, pp. 181-205.

41 Giegerich, *The Soul's Logical Life*, p. 204.

course, to the mythical huntsman who when he came upon the goddess Artemis whilst sojourning in the wilderness was instantly transformed into a stag and torn apart by his own hunting dogs. And surely, it was with this myth in mind that Hegel wrote his famous words about negation and dismemberment as mediators of truth:

> But the life of the Spirit is not the life that shrinks from death and keeps itself untouched by devastation, but rather the life that endures it and maintains itself in it. It wins its truth only when, in utter dismemberment, it finds itself. It is this power, not as something positive, which closes its eyes to the negative as when we say of something that it is nothing or is false, and then having done with it, turn away and pass on to something else; on the contrary, spirit is this power only by looking the negative in the face, and tarrying with it. This tarrying with the negative is the magical power that converts it into being.[42]

What I am driving at here is that even though Marlan has not caught up with his textual vision's initiating him into what in PDI we call logical negativity, *he has had that vision.* He has seen the dog that is not a dog, the conceptual, noetic, linguistic Curtis. Why, it may even be said that the true Curtis of his text jumps from the page where the death of his actual dog is described, like the vision Jung spoke of looming up out of the ordinary. Never mind that Marlan tightens up against it as something quoted from me with which he disagrees.[43] It has clearly cut into him, gotten under his skin, compelled him to tarry with it. And this could not have

---

[42] G. W. F. Hegel, *Phenomenology of Spirit,* trans. A. V. Miller, Oxford: Oxford University Press, 1977, p. 19.

[43] Perhaps, I am too lenient here. Can it really be allowed to pass that a *psychologist* tightens up in his personhood from the soul truth that has shown itself? For a more rigorous examination of such a "sin against the Spirit(!)," this time exemplified by Jung's dream of himself as being unable to bow his head all the way to the floor when he found himself before the Highest Presence, see Wolfgang Giegerich, "Jung's Millimeter: Feigned Submission—Clandestine Defiance: Jung's Religious Psychology," *CEP*, vol. VI, pp. 3-46.

happened had he not ventured into the wild as did Actaion in the myth I mentioned.

Now, of course, the wild of the myth just referred to is an allusion to Giegerich's use of this image as a way of figuring the absolute negativity that consciousness or "the soul" simultaneously attains and gives rise to when it relentlessly exposes itself to what is. Said another way, the wild is an image of interiority, of the soul as absolute-negative interiority. And it is with this meaning in mind that Giegerich makes the important point that the interiority of the soul is not to be thought of as the inside of something external which it is surrounded and transcended by, but as having (at least for the still imaginally-based mind) an epiphanic character. In "The Epiphany of Artemis" chapter of his *The Soul's Logical Life* (and I should say that it is this chapter that Marlan was alluding to when he chided Giegerich with finding truth by chasing a naked Goddess), Giegerich explains that

> … as long as the wilderness appears only as an infinite expanse all around you to which you are exposed, you still see it somehow from outside! Paradoxically, you are not really in it yet, despite having (seemingly) ventured into it and being surrounded by it on all sides. Wilderness as vastness, as contourless wall of otherness, is still an abstraction. It is the simple (undialectical) negation of the positive, domesticated sphere. It is not yet the negative, determinate nought (HEGEL) of the fenced-in realm (negation of the negation). You have positively left the realm of positivity and positively (physically or imaginally) entered the wilderness, but you still behold it from the standpoint of positivity that you brought along with you into the alleged wild. Once you are really in the wild, it also shows itself as Artemis. Artemis is nothing else but the further determination of the notion of 'wilderness,' the revelation of its inner image or mystery.[44]

It is the last lines of this passage, which I already cited in my earlier essay, that I want especially to emphasize. Transposing them into

---

[44] Giegerich, *The Soul's Logical Life*, p. 215.

the terms of what it is my purpose to show here, the implication is clear: the dying Curtis of Marlan's text is nothing else than the further determination of his analytical psychology, the revelation of its inner image or mystery. It is because Marlan has really entered the wild of analytical psychology by engaging in a cutting-edge and high-level theoretical dispute that, win that dispute or lose it (it matters little which[45]), it shows itself to him as Curtis.

But what more precisely does it mean to say that in the wild of his dispute with Giegerich analytical psychology shows itself to Marlan as Curtis the dog? With this question we come to the crux of Marlan's and Giegerich's differences with respect to the so-called unassimilable remainder or remnant. For Marlan, as we have already discussed, our consciousness and psychic life are ultimately humbled and thrown back upon themselves by an unthinkable and unknowable otherness that he variously describes as "a residue, a *caput mortuum*, … an archetypally cumbersome object, a real limit, which remains and unhinges the elevating process of spirit on its path to return into itself in absolute interiority."[46] Which is why he rejected my "conceptual, noetic, linguistic dog" and clings to the ashes left in the retort, the remains of his physical dog. For Giegerich, by contrast, no image, symbol, symptom, or psychological phenomenon is unthinkable, unknowable. For although the ego may indeed be humbled by it (where it has not already been departed from to produce the psychological standpoint), the subject matter, whatever that may be, is nothing else than the soul's own thought, even if not yet in the form of thought. Which is of course why interpretation (i.e., the thinking of such thoughts by and as psychology) is needed. "What nature leaves imperfect, the Art perfects," states the alchemical motto.

[45] Just as Hegel taught that the infinite and the finite are not simple opposites, bordering upon each other (which would limit, and thus contradict the concept of the infinite), so too winning and losing are not alternatives that exclude each other, but co-determining aspects of one another.

[46] Marlan, "The absolute that is not absolute," p. 1.

With these reflections we come to a critical juncture. The interpretation I have given thus far—of Marlan's dog story as reflecting his disillusionment and grief over the loss of pet theories and theorists—could have been made by any analytic psychotherapist. Each day in their consulting rooms therapists from various schools of analysis routinely hear references to third parties, or to topics and subject areas that are seemingly external to the matter at hand, as displacements. You don't need to have studied PDI to hear Marlan's moving description of the death of Curtis as indicative of the feelings of loss he has repressed with respect to Jung, Hillman, and analytical psychology having gone under for him, especially not when his report about this experience is given in an article in which traditional Jungian thought is being defended from successionist versions of that thought. PDI is only needed for what comes next, that is, for thinking Marlan's report about the euthanized Curtis as a statement of the soul (we could also say, of psychology) about itself.

Turning to this now, and in the interests of placing the interpretive onus on what I have been calling Marlan's PDI,[47] let us begin with the cryptic, alchemy-like sentence from the philosopher, John Sallis, which Marlan places as an epigraph at the top of the essay he wrote prior in the series to the one we are discussing here. "It will be a matter," declares Sallis, "… of attempting to say things in a way that lets the shining of their stone be manifest, [and this, moreover, in a way] that lets be manifest what is gathered into that shining."[48] Adapting this statement to our present purpose, the interpretative challenge of Marlan's PDI may similarly be described as one of thinking in a way that lets the shining essence of the euthanized Curtis (what Marlan in his text calls the "mixture of grief, love, and wonder"

---

[47] His implicit, unwitting, but dialectically inevitable PDI.

[48] Cited by Marlan in "From the Black Sun to the Philosophers' Stone," *Spring 74*, p. 1.

that the cremated remains of Curtis continue to fill him with) be manifest, and this in a manner that at the same time "lets be manifest what is gathered into that shining."

But what does it mean to think in this *manifesting-the-shine-that-lets-be-manifest-what-is-gathered-into-that-shine* manner? Without going into all that I explained in the previous essay of mine that Marlan referred to in order to bring his dog into the discussion, it is a matter of a speculative style of thinking in which all the predicates of a text or life situation are read, not merely as quality predicates, but as essential ones that upon a careful reading and re-reading of the whole, change-up our grasp of what the subject was thought to be in the first place.[49] Outside his text, Marlan, as was pointed out before, is a psychologist who, in addition to being that, owns a dog. Curtis, likewise, was a dog who in addition to being that, died. In both cases, there is nothing in these facts that is essential, nothing that brings out "the shine of their stone," let alone anything that makes manifest what all is "gathered in that shining." Not even their bond as dog and master does this. Lovely as it may be, it is just another quality predicate, like colour and breed, temperament, etc. True, it may well be that their lives together have changed each other up such that as subjects they have been returned to themselves by their otherness. Yes, of course that is the case. But nevertheless, what I said still holds. They fall outside one another's essential nature, which is in keeping, I suppose, with Marlan's (strangely ambivalent!) emphasis upon unassimilable otherness, externality.

How different, however, is the Curtis of Marlan's text! All that is needed in order to think in the aforementioned *manifesting-the-shine-that-lets-be-manifest-what-is-gathered-into-that-shine* manner is to realize that *this* Curtis is not a living creature who

---

[49] For Hegel's main discussion of the philosophical proposition or speculative sentence see his *Phenomenology of Spirit* § 62-63, p. 39. See also pages 13-14 above.

in addition to that is subsequently euthanized, but is *euthanized from the outset*—not a dog that additionally and subsequent to the life it lived has died, but wagged by Death as by its own tail, a self-negating, self-sublating dog of death or death-dog. So much, then, for the manifesting-of-the-shine part of the dialectic of interpretation I am calling Marlan's PDI. Having accounted for the dark-light that the textual Curtis manifests by being negated from the outset, we have to also think this shine in a way *that-lets-be-manifest-what-is-gathered-into-that-shine.* And what, or rather, who is it that is gathered into that shine? We already dully know, but now must know again via the dark-light of the shine that the Euthanized-from-the-outset Curtis of Marlan's text brings to analytical psychology, that it is none other than those analytic forebearers, Jung and Hillman, whose loss Marlan unconsciously displaced onto his deceased pet. Curtis, it follows, is the *result* of their passing away, the *result* of their having become historical for us—why, we might even say: a downright successionist cur! And here now, as I write these words, the speculative meaning of Marlan's dog story becomes clear to me in a flash. Whereas Marlan, lagging behind his own story, clings to Jung and Hillman via his resistance to successionist developments of Jungian thought, the euthanized Curtis of his text is nothing else than the resolution of this transference come (immanently, critically) home to itself, which is also to say, the unleashing of that hound of heaven, animus psychology!

It is like when Hegel, thinking the negation of the negation in his famous Speculative Remark, differentiates between the sublatedness that is brought about by negation, on the one hand, and nothing, on the other. The meaning of sublation "must be grasped with precision and especially distinguished from *nothing*.—What is sublated does not thereby turn into nothing. Nothing is *immediate*; something sublated is on the contrary something mediated; it is something non-existent but as a result that has proceeded from a being; it still *has in itself*, therefore, the *determinateness from which it derives*."[50] Making the same point in terms of Marlan's article we can say much the same of the dog that appears in its pages. This Curtis, too, although something non-existent, is "a result that proceeded from a being," that is, a logically negative shine. And he is this, moreover, in a manner that "still has in [himself] ... the determinateness from which [he] derives." Which is as much as to say (and let it be appreciated that in saying this I am at the same time underscoring the line that Marlan quoted from Sallis about *manifesting-the-shine-that-lets-be-manifest-what-is-gathered-into-that-shine*), that the Euthanized-from-the outset dog of Marlan's article is the sublated result, or in his words, "mongrel mix," of all the forebearers, thinkers, theories, and arguments in his text. Jung, Hillman, Giegerich; Kant, Hegel, Jacobi, Sallis; "the thing considered as it is in itself," "the unassimilable remainder," "the archetypally cumbersome object," etc.: without these, no Curtis, even as without Curtis, not this particular mongrel mix.

The point I am making—about the Euthanized-from-the-outset Curtis being the sublated or mongrel result of the determinateness from which he derives—is pretty much the same as the point Borges makes in his charming little essay, "Kafka's Precursors." After assembling a list of previous authors whose works in one way or another can be claimed to anticipate Kafka's authorship, Borges wonders at the remarkable fact that most of these authors have nothing else in common.

> If I am not mistaken, the heterogeneous pieces I have enumerated resemble Kafka; if I am not mistaken, not all of

---

[50] G. W. F. Hegel, *The Science of Logic*, trans. George Di Giovanni, Cambridge: Cambridge University Press, 2010, p. 81.

> them resemble each other. This second fact is the most significant. In each of these texts we find Kafka's idiosyncrasy to a greater or lesser degree, but if Kafka had never written a line, we would not perceive this quality; in other words, it would not exist.[51]

And so it is for Marlan's precursors. If he had not given to our literature his story about Curtis's death, that quality of his authorship that brings the aforementioned authors and ideas together would not have been able to do so. The unity of their unity and difference would not be thought in this Marlanesque, dog-making manner. And it is the same the other way around. Without their appearing in his article, no story about Curtis. And this, moreover, may be reckoned to be so even by his own lights. For as we know, doing justice to his relationship with Curtis is the criterion he insists upon for both human relevance and psychological truth.

But, then again, on second thoughts I have to say that this is not quite right. For, on the *psychic* side of the psychological difference, Marlan tightens up against and turns back from what I am ascribing to him on the *psychological* side of that difference. He complains, as we have already heard, that for his PDI colleagues (and remember that his specific reference is to the previous article of mine that prompted him to relate his dog story in the first place) "the 'actual' other is dismissed and my dog becomes my mind and my mind my dog." It is this, he says, that "does not satisfy me, nor account for the reality of my relationship with Curtis."[52] But is it not rather the case that the reality of his relationship with his actual dog, Curtis, does not satisfy what Jung called the "[other] picture [that] looms up, covered by a thin veil of actual facts," i.e., the Euthanized-from-

---

[51] Jorge Luis Borges, *Labyrinths: Selected Stories & Other Writings*, New York: New Directions Books, 1962, p. 201.

[52] Marlan, "The absolute that is not absolute," p. 6.

the-outset soul-dog of his text, which has visioned itself forth as the seeing from within of his high-level dispute with Giegerich and PDI?[53]

Marlan, it seems to me, flees his PDI, much as the figure of the I in dreams so often flees the figure(s) of its other. But this, it may be claimed, is already the *coniunctio*—or so, I submit, his dismembered oneness with the Euthanized-from-the-outset-Curtis-of-his-text can be read to reflect. Of course, I do not by any means want to force this reading upon Marlan. I am only trying to show, "bone of my bone, flesh of my flesh," how (having met myself in Marlan!) I see things. I fully agree with Jung that the analyst should not be too zealous in his efforts on behalf of his patients and should even respect their right to go to the dogs if they must.[54]

Going to the dogs, however, has here a double meaning. Marlan goes to, clings to, "his 'actual' dog." He tells us about what *he* thinks and feels about the dog that he had to put down. He does not tell us what the Euthanized-from-the-outset Curtis of his dog story thinks. Reflecting upon this shortcoming, I am put in mind of Giegerich's advisement that, "A psychology that keeps psychological phenomena *attached* to the human being as '*his* psychology' is on the leash of the person *as* person." An important point. Many cities have by-laws requiring dogs to be held on their master's leash even as they have sometimes special areas called off-leash parks. But should psychology be bound by such a by-law? Should it not rather unleash its dog, think without restraints? Continuing his criticism, Giegerich writes,

---

[53] In a deeply insightful discussion of the psychological difference at play in Jung's style of interpretation, Giegerich makes the point that "To take the stories, memories, dream images, and other psychic productions seriously only for the patient's sake, that is, only because one wants to understand and help *him*, but not because one wants to understand *them* in their substance and in their truth, is at bottom the most hurtful betrayal, the greatest disparagement." His "The Provenance of C. G. Jung's Psychological Findings," *CEP,* vol. I, pp. 137-142. See also his *The Soul's Logical Life*, pp. 71-72.

[54] C. G. Jung, *CW* 18 ¶ 291-295.

> As pathological and destructive as those psychological phenomena may be for the empirical person [and here let us recall the "experiences of brokenness, incision, wound, castration, cut[,] negation, and … ultimate 'no' to consciousness" that Marlan mentions—G.M.], they are nonetheless never allowed to turn against his ontological status as a person (an entity) and tear this status apart, because his personness serves as the by definition unaffected containing vessel for an otherwise possibly turbulent, maybe even disastrous process. Psychology itself is likewise protected against being torn apart by its own subject matter, against being decomposed (sublated) by the soul as logical negativity …, because it is conceived as the unaffected containing vessel for 'psychological reality.'[55]

Returning from here to Marlan's account of his having held his dog as it died: is this story as he tells it not the even sadder story of the curbing of his "psychology's need to be torn apart by its own subject matter" and to be "decomposed (sublated) by the soul as logical negativity"? I can say for myself that I think that it is, but also note, as I said above, that it counts towards the initiatory dismemberment of his psychological stance that he has had that vision.

*   *   *

For my final reflection I want say a little more about the speculative meaning of Marlan's dog story. As I mentioned above, while I was reading and re-reading Marlan's article it became clear to me in a flash that the Euthanized Curtis of his text reflects the resolution of the transference come home to itself. Now by "transference" I mean in this context having an identity position as Jungian which clings to Jung, Hillman, Giegerich, or some other forebear in much the same manner as Marlan (in an article explicitly taking a stand against successionist developments!) describes

[55] Giegerich, *The Soul's Logical Life*, p. 212.

himself as clinging to Curtis. And by "resolution of the transference come home to itself" I mean pretty much what that sentence that has traditionally been ascribed to Aristotle declares, "I love Plato, but truth I love even more," which Giegerich with admirable felicity has cited with Jung in mind.[56] It follows from this that the Euthanized-from-the-outset Curtis looming up from within Marlan's text signifies the resolution of this transference, that is, the achieved (though in his article and by him reneged upon) capacity of the psychologist to cut the leash and think psychology forward on his own responsibility. No need for that Old Yeller of an "unassimilable remnant" to vouchsafe the stature of Jung, et al., as unsucceedable, insurmountable. Euthanized-from-the-outset (which is also to say, recognized as having become historical for us), our forebearers' legacy can be *thought*, and this, moreover, in a way that while loving them, loves truth more. It is what Hegel was getting at with his aforementioned Speculative Remark. "[The thinking that arises from sublation] does not thereby turn into nothing … , but as a result that has proceeded from a being[,] it still *has in itself*, therefore, the *determinateness from which it derives*."[57] The Jungian spirit, likewise, carries on via a successive series of immanent self-critiques, the Curtis of Marlan's dog story as animus psychology. It is a matter, as I said, of the resolution of the transference come home to itself, i.e., of a Jungian psychology that, having "negated the basis from which it starts," has by that same means "ascend[ed] to what is truly self-subsistent and self-explanatory"[58]: Analytical Psychology in the twenty-first century.

---

[56] Giegerich, Personal email to author, February 20, 2005.

[57] G. W. F. Hegel, *The Science of Logic*, trans. George Di Giovanni, Cambridge: Cambridge University Press, 2010, p. 81.

[58]. John N. Findlay, "Foreword," In G. W. F. Hegel, *Hegel's Logic: Being Part One of the Encyclopedia of Philosophical Sciences*, trans. William Wallace, Oxford: Clarendon Press, 1975. The full quote is cited above on page 60.

About the Author

Greg Mogenson is a registered psychotherapist and Jungian psychoanalyst practicing in London, Ontario, Canada. He is a founding member and current Vice-President of The International Society for Psychology as the Discipline of Interiority. The author of numerous articles in the field of analytical psychology, his books include *Psychology's Dream of the Courtroom*; *A Most Accursed Religion: When a Trauma becomes God*; *Greeting the Angels: An Imaginal View of the Mourning Process*; *The Dove in the Consulting Room: Hysteria and the Anima in Bollas and Jung*; *Northern Gnosis: Thor, Baldr, and the Volsungs in the Thought of Freud and Jung*, and (with W. Giegerich and D. L. Miller) *Dialectics & Analytical Psychology: The El Capitan Canyon Seminar*. He is also the author to two other essays in the ISPDI Monograph Series, *Dereliction of Duty and the Rise of Psychology, as Reflected in the "Case" of Conrad's Lord Jim* and *That Glimpse of Truth for which you had Forgotten to Ask*.

For further information, visit the website at: www.gregmogenson.com

www.ingramcontent.com/pod-product-compliance
Ingram Content Group UK Ltd.
Pitfield, Milton Keynes, MK11 3LW, UK
UKHW041642190726
13854UKWH00006B/2649